Discover Your Power

A Practical Approach to Bible-Based Meditation

Derrick Traylor

Healing House Publishing Co.
Where Your Voice Can Be Read

PORTLAND, OREGON

Discover Your Power, A Practical Approach to Bible-Based Meditation
Copyright © 2011 by Dr. Derrick Traylor

All Rights Reserved. Except as permitted under the U.S. Copyright Act of 1976, No part of this book may be reproduced, stored or transmitted in any form or by any means, electronic or mechanical, including photocopying and recording, or by any information storage or retrieval system, except as may be expressly permitted in writing by the publisher. Requests for permission should be addressed in writing to:

OC/O Healing House Publishing LLC
Derrick Traylor
4803 SE 64th Ave
Portland, OR 97206

First edition, January 2012
ISBN SOFTCOVER: 978-0-9847705-0-2

Unless otherwise noted, Scripture quotations are taken from *Holy Bible, New International Version*®. Copyright © 1973, 1978, 1984 by International Bible Society. Used by permission of Zondervan Publishing House.

Scripture quotations marked (KJV) are taken from *The Holy Bible: King James Version*. This is in the Public Domain and there are no copyright restrictions.

Scripture quotations marked (NKJV) are taken from the *New King James Version*. Copyright 1979, 1980, 1982 by Thomas Nelson, inc. Used by permission. All rights reserved.

Scripture quotations marked herein (NRSV) are from the *New Revised Standard Version Bible*, Copyright © 1989, Division of Christian Education of the National Council of Christ in the U.S.A., and are used by permission. All rights reserved.

Scripture taken from *The Amplified Bible, Old Testament* copyright © 1965, 1987 by the Zondervan Corporation. *The Amplified New Testament* copyright © 1958, 1987 by The Lockman Foundation. Used by permission.

10 9 8 7 6 5 4 3 2 1

Cover Design by Adazing Design (www.adazing.com)
Interior Book Design by Coreen Montagna (coreenm@gmail.com)
Editor: Ryan Adair (www.missiowriting.com)
Research Assistants: Kathy and Matt Teel (www.teelwriting.com)
Photography: Emily Andrews Portrait Design (www.EmilyAndrews.com)

Printed in the United States of America

*This book is dedicated to my Father which is in heaven, Jesus Christ.
It is in him that I live, move, and have my being.
I am grateful to be a son of God.*

Table of Contents

SECTION 1
Meditation

CHAPTER 1 3
The Importance of the Bible

- *Basic Assumptions*
- *Divine Purposes*
- *Beneficiaries of God's Wealth*
- *Reverence for God's Word*
- *Getting Our Priorities Right*

CHAPTER 2 13
The Process of Think, Say, See, and Be

- *Listening to God's Gentle Voice*
- *Defining Meditation*
- *Think, See, Say, and Be*
- *Biblical Example of the Think, See, Say, and Be Process*
- *The Pain and Pressure of the Process*

CHAPTER 3 25
Meditation's Attributes and Benefits

- *Meditation in Action*
- *Sacred Space*
- *Focused Silence*
- *A Form of Prayer*
- *Meditation's Benefits*
- *Meditation Prepares the Heart*

CHAPTER 4 35
The Reasons and Practicalities of Meditation

- *Your Internal Conversation*
- *Why Do People Meditate?*
- *A Time and a Place*
- *Practice*

CHAPTER 5 45
The Biblical Mandate

- *Meditation Throughout the Old Testament*
- *Meditation Throughout the Psalms*
- *Meditation Throughout the New Testament*

CHAPTER 6 53
Myths, Facts, and the Patterns of God

- *Common Misunderstandings*
- *Meditation, Recitation, and Manifestation*
- *Recitation Steps*
- *Manifestation of the Dream*
- *The Role of Faith in Meditation*

A NOTE TO THE READER..65
A Prophetic Message

SECTION 2
Recitation

CHAPTER 7 69
Forming the Habit and the Warfare Within

- *Developing a Habit*
- *Talk to Your Spouse*
- *Active Resistance*
- *The Warfare Within*
- *Effectual Prayer*

CHAPTER 8 77
A Checklist for Fruitful Meditation

- *Personal Example of Meditation*
- *Checklist for Fruitful Meditation*
- *Tips on Meditating*

CHAPTER 9 89
Types of Meditation: Needs, "Mantras," Objects, and Mindfulness

- *Different Types of Meditation*
- *Differing Needs*
- *A Willing Heart—No Method*
- *Counting Breaths*
- *Mantra: Repeating a Praise Word*
- *Meditating on an Object*
- *Mindfulness*

CHAPTER 10 103
Types of Meditation: Biblical Meditation

- *Lectio Divina (Divine Reading)*
- *Meditating on a Bible Passage*
- *Meditating on a Bible Verse*
- *Visualization: Placing Yourself in the Scene*
- *Visualization: Imagining God's Future Acts*

CHAPTER 11 117
Types of Meditation: Music, Self-Examination, and Wrestling with Demons

- *Meditating with Music*
- *Self-Examination and Repentance*
- *Wrestling with Angels and Demons*

CHAPTER 12 129
Types of Meditation: Virtue, Fasting, and Meditational Walking

- *Meditating on Virtue*
- *Meditation and Fasting*
- *Walking Meditation*

SECTION 3
Manifestation

CHAPTER 13 141
Meditation's Physical Benefits

- What is Manifestation?
- Physical Benefits
- Body-Benefits

CHAPTER 14 155
The Psychological, Relational, and Spiritual Benefits of Meditation

- Good for Our Minds
- Psychological and Behavioral Problems
- Good for Our Emotions
- Good for Our Relationships
- Spiritual Benefits of Meditation

CHAPTER 15 169
Falling Deeper in Love with Jesus Christ

- The Gifts of the Holy Spirit
- Deeper Love of God: A More Intimate Relationship with Him
- Deeper Willingness to Act: More Access to the Power of God to Act

APPENDIX A 185
Words to Use as a Mantra

• Names of Jesus • Names for God the Father •
• Names for the Holy Spirit •Attributes of God •

APPENDIX B 191
Phrases to Use as a Mantra

APPENDIX C 193
Bible Verses to Meditate On

• For Strength • For Comfort • For Repentance •
• For Discernment • For Needs • For Gratitude •
• For Acceptance of God's Will •

APPENDIX D 203
Passages for Visualization

Acknowledgments

I learned long ago that no one does anything great alone. God in his wisdom sends amazing people into your life who are assigned to help you realize your dream. There are so many people who have helped to make this book a reality. First, I want to say thank you to my wonderful wife Angela for being so loving and supportive of my vision and ministry. Thank you for having such a caring heart. I appreciate your support and understanding through the countless late night and early morning writing sessions. Sometimes you waited up for me and sometimes you didn't, but thank you anyway. LOL. Angela, you are an awesome woman, wife, mom, and physician. The world is better because you are here. I love you!

To my Prince Judah — you inspire me every day to be a better man, husband, and dad. I love you, son. You are incredible. Thank you for greeting me at the door with a great big "DAAADDYYY!" after I have had a long day of work at the church. Your hug and kiss makes everything better. Although you quickly return to watch Nick Jr., I know you love me and that makes all the difference.

To my mom, Mary Lewis, for being such a strong woman, full of faith and love. Your strength and resilience has taught me so much. Thanks for raising all six of us kids by yourself. You taught us to be strong, independent, prayerful, and hard working. I am the strong man I am today because of you. I love you very much Mom!

To my dad, Tommie Sr. — thanks for expressing the love and pride that you have for us.

All of my siblings are very special to me as well. Cynthia, you are one of kind. I am proud to call you my big sister. Thanks for sharing the burden of ministry with Angie and I. You have the unique ability to vacillate between the roles of big sister and spiritual daughter without violating either. You're the greatest!

Tommie Jr., you are a great big brother. You are always a phone call away. Thanks for encouraging me to do all that is in my heart. You have a way of making all of us feel safe. I love you!

Alvin, "Al," your heart is amazing. Thanks for remembering everybody's birthday, and making sure we are alright. You make us remember what's important. I remember one summer you worked so I would have money to go on a church youth trip. I never forgot that. Thanks for your gift of loving and caretaking.

Martell, as my baby brother you hold a special place in my heart. You are great beyond your wildest imagination. Thanks for being a faithful musician at our church. You are truly one of the best drummers I know. I love you very much!

Carolyn, "Carol," my little baby sister we all love you so much. You have such a caring heart and a kind spirit. Thanks for making me laugh. Your witty personality brings so much light to us all. You are a young woman of great wealth and strength. I love you.

Gente', DeMorees, DJ, and Tommie III — your uncle loves you very much. Thanks for being there for me.

Finally, to my staff and the entire family of Rehoboth World Healing Center, I love every one of you. Thanks for trusting me as your pastor and spiritual father. I am grateful to have been chosen to lead such an august body of believers.

Section One
Meditation

*Meditation is the tongue of the soul
and the language of our spirit.*

—Jeremy Taylor (1613–1667)

Chapter 1

The Importance of the Bible

O Lord, thou hast made us for Thyself,
and our hearts are restless until they rest in Thee.
—Augustine, Bishop of Hippo in North Africa (354–430)

So let us make a commitment to meditation—to ponder, reflect, memorize, and to imagine this Word—so we can move forward and begin to recite the Word, preach the Word, and receive the revelation of the Word of God through meditation. It is time to kill everything that's not like you, Lord. Kill the works of the flesh so the Spirit of God can rule and reign in our lives, hearts, and relationships.

Basic Assumptions

This is a book about Christian meditation—meditation on the Word of God. There's no place God reveals himself more clearly than through his words given to us in the Bible. To meditate on that Word is to let the Lord into your heart more deeply, more fully, every day. It's to let him in so completely, that after a while there's not much room for anything that isn't God, or at least of God.

Believers aren't the only people who meditate, of course, but there are some things I'm going to assume about you if you're reading this book. I assume you are a Christian. You don't have to be the same kind of Christian as me, but I am going to assume you love the Lord Jesus, you believe in his name, you've been saved, and you want to grow closer to him—desires all Christians have, no matter what church they attend. As I teach you how to get closer to him through meditation, I'm going to assume you want those things too.

If you're not a believer, that's also okay. You might be a seeker, searching for the place where your heart can find rest. The Lord honors your quest to find him. He's given each of us a path to walk with a promise that he's not only at the end of the path *for* us, but on the path *with* us—he *is* the path beneath our feet, holding us up and keeping us from falling. "I am the way," he promises us.[1] Within these pages you will find helpful tools you can use to strengthen your faith because, after all, meditation is beneficial for everyone.

Divine Purposes

I want you to realize that you did not end up with this book by accident but by the divine purpose of God. He has an awesome plan for your life; and it might just be that your journey begins here, with the teaching you now hold in your hand. "'For I know the plans I have for you,' declares the Lord, 'plans to prosper you and not to harm you, plans to give you hope and a future'" (Jeremiah 29:11).

---

1. See John 14:6

I don't know what led you to where you are at this very moment. For some people it's a broken, troubled road that leads to the moment of invitation into the presence of God. No matter what your current state is, God's grace is available to you.

Whatever your sins are or whatever your past is, and whatever others have done to hurt you, hear the promise of God for your life: your history does not determine your destiny. Rather, your history becomes the school through which you have matriculated. The awesome lessons learned from your past experiences have prepared you to fulfill your God-given purpose. God predestined you to live for him and be his ambassador before the foundation of the world. If you really listen, you can hear God telling you the same thing he told Jeremiah many years ago: "Before I formed you in the womb I knew you, before you were born I set you apart; I appointed you as a prophet to the nations" (Jeremiah 1:5).

It doesn't matter how you were conceived, God had a specific purpose for you. It doesn't matter who your parents are, God has a purpose for you. Your purpose may not be prophetic like Jeremiah's; but I can guarantee that whatever your call is, it is great in God's eyes.

The Holy Spirit will enlighten and empower you as you continue to read this book. Through meditating on the Word of God your future will be full of victory as the promises of God are manifested in your life.

Beneficiaries of God's Wealth

If you are a Christian, it is my assumption that you understand the important role the Bible plays in the life of a believer. Every Christian should hold the Word of God as the centerpiece of his or her life. It is your guide, teacher, and your most direct connection to the thoughts and will of God. Anyone who seeks to be close to God must be a student of his Word.

There are two Greek words that mean *word*, or more specifically, *the word of God* they are *logos* and *rhema*. *Logos* is the written Word of God, also known as the Bible. *Rhema* is the spoken word, a special revelation or insight to someone concerning a matter that is not clearly covered in Scripture. *Rhema* can also be characterized by a deeper understanding of a particular verse or passage that results in immediate application to address a current situation. As a believer you should daily seek a *rhema* for guidance.

As sons and daughters of God we are beneficiaries of the wealth that is found in his Word. In terms of inheritance, the Bible becomes the binding testament of God to reveal how he wants his estate to be divided among his children. And it's a big estate; it encompasses the entire earth, even the entire universe. This is why David wrote: "The earth is the Lord's, and everything in it, the world, and all who live in it" (Psalm 24:1).

Paul confirms that we are rightful heirs to his kingdom through Christ in his letter to the Romans:

> Because those who are led by the Spirit of God are sons of God. For you did not receive a spirit that makes you a slave again to fear, but you received the Spirit of sonship. And by him we cry, "*Abba*, Father." The Spirit himself testifies with our spirit that we are God's children. Now if we are children, then we are heirs—heirs of God and co-heirs with Christ, if indeed we share in his sufferings in order that we may also share in his glory. (Romans 8:14–17)

"Abba, Father" here denotes "source and sustainer." Just like a good earthly father is not only the creator but the sustainer of his child's life, so God both creates and sustains the lives of his children. Therefore, as a son or daughter of God, you must embrace your sonship and know that God desires to give you all good things which pertain to life and godliness. James reminds us of this when he writes, "Don't be deceived, my dear brothers. Every good and perfect gift is from above, coming down from the Father of the heavenly lights, who does not change like shifting shadows" (1:16–17).

Sometimes a sister in Christ gets a little upset at being told to embrace her *sonship*—after all, how can ladies ever claim to be sons? But back when the New Testament was being written, daughters could never inherit their fathers' wealth. A daughter could not be the heiress of a kingdom, a home, or even the money she needed to live on. Only a son could be the heir. But our Lord came and offered the status of sonship—that right to claim every blessing of the Father and to be his legitimate heir—to both his brothers *and* his sisters, men *and* women who believed. So you who are daughters of the Father, to claim your sonship is to claim your inheritance.

Sadly, many believers are living beneath their privilege as children of God because they do not know what their benefits are. Many believers have lived and died—full of hope, dreams, visions, and aspirations—not knowing they are heirs and heiresses of God. All they had ever dreamed of was already at their disposal through the Word of God; but they did not know how to access it.

But God has a greater desire for you. As you continue to read this book, you will learn how to access the promises of God through meditating on his Word, which is always relevant to your need.

David describes some of those needs in Psalm 103:2–7:

> Praise the Lord, O my soul, and forget not all his benefits—who forgives all your sins and heals all your diseases, who redeems your life from the pit and crowns you with love and compassion, who satisfies your desires with good things so that your youth is renewed like the eagle's. The Lord works righteousness and justice for all the oppressed. He made known his ways to Moses, his deeds to the people of Israel.

You must never forget that, as a son or daughter of God, you are royalty, highly favored by God. It is time for you to take advantage of your benefits. Start now by praying this prayer:

> *Father, in the name of Jesus, I acknowledge your sovereign reign and rule over all creation—in heaven, earth, and under the earth. There is no God like you. I thank you for your grace that was extended to me at Calvary. I thank you for allowing your grace to cover me daily. Father, I repent before you now for any and all sins I have committed, whether they were things I shouldn't have done but did, or things I should have done but failed to do. I ask you to cleanse me now that I might be accepted into your presence. In your presence is fullness of joy and at your right hand are pleasures forevermore. My soul longs for the joy that only you can give; so Father I receive your joy now in Jesus' name.*
>
> *Today, I also pray for the Spirit of wisdom, knowledge, understanding, and revelation to be upon me, that I might learn your laws and precepts to live a successful life through your Word. Father, your Word declares that I should meditate on it day and night. So Lord, please give me a hunger and thirst for your Word, and that I will be transformed into the image of your Son.*
>
> *Father, in the name of Jesus and according to your divine power, you have given me everything I need for life and godliness. All I need to receive those things is to know you. Enlighten the eyes of my understanding that*

I may know what is the hope of your calling, and what are the riches of your inheritance.

I pray that you would allow my mind to be renewed by your Word daily. Now, in the name of Jesus, I take authority over every deaf and dumb spirit, every mind-binding spirit of oppression. I now totally commit my ways to the you so that my thoughts would be established. In Jesus' name I have a love for the Word of God, my conscious mind is alert and ready to receive the new paradigm given by his Word. I am now ready to walk into my divine destiny through Christ Jesus.

In Jesus' name, amen!

Reverence for God's Word

I was once asked by a non-Christian, "Why do you have such a reverence for the Bible?"

"There are many reasons," I responded, "but I will share two of the most important ones. First, I believe the Bible is the infallible Word of God; inspired by God and written by men of God. Secondly, and most importantly, I reverence and obey the Word of God because it reveals God through Jesus Christ, who is God manifested in the flesh."

I was talking about the truth of God in Christ that we find throughout the Bible, but is clearest in the beginning of John's gospel: "In the beginning was the Word, and the Word was with God, and the Word was God. He was with God in the beginning. Through him all things were made; without him nothing was made that has been made" (John 1:1–3). Then again: "The Word became flesh and made his dwelling among us. We have seen his glory, the glory of the One and Only, who came from the Father, full of grace and truth" (John 1:14).

This passage shows us a powerful revelation: the Word that was God (vs. 1) is the same Word that became flesh and dwelt among us (vs. 14). The flesh that dwelt among us was given a name that was above every other name—the name of Jesus. Now then, when you meditate on the Word you are meditating on God, because Jesus himself is God the Son. And you meditate in the power and protection of God, as well, because the Holy Spirit is God working in your life and heart, and he will never abandon you.

Getting Our Priorities Right

To help you understand meditation, I will build on the fundamental understanding of prayer. Prayer is simply a conversation with God. And we know that whatever we ask in his name and according to his Word will be done for us: "This is the confidence we have in approaching God: that if we ask anything according to his will, he hears us. And if we know that he hears us—whatever we ask—we know that we have what we asked of him (1 John 5:14–15).

Contrary to popular belief, effective prayer is not determined by enticing words; there's no magic formula that will make God bestow blessings on you if you say it in just the right way. But rather, a prayer made up of faith-filled words and an obedient heart is what will win God's approval. If you are like me you can't make it through one day without saying, "Please, God," "Lord, have mercy," or "Lord, help me!" Each day we can ask for protection for our loved ones, and for patience, strength, or comfort for ourselves. God always responds to even the fewest words as long as they are faith-filled.

The presence of the Lord is the only place you can go where everything negative ceases to exist. No sickness, disease, frustration, stress, worry, doubt, or fear can stand in the presence of the Lord. In his presence is fullness of joy. David found the place of great delight, joy, and comfort: "you will fill me with joy in your presence, with eternal pleasures at your right hand" (Psalm 16:11).

It can often be a challenge to get quiet long enough to meditate on God and his Word. Nevertheless, you must learn to value the presence of God more than you value anything else. Television, the Internet, cell phones—all these can become distractions and time thieves. They are used as devices to make you miss your divine moments with God and the provisions he has made for you.

You must ask yourself a serious question: What do you want the most? Entertainment or change? Once you begin to put some things into perspective in your life, with God always being first, you will become anxious to spend time with the Father on a daily basis.

In a world filled with gadgets, electronics, social networks, and so many other distractions, it can be next to impossible to find consistent time every day to commune with God. But I promise if you do, your quality of life will improve drastically. God does not ask you for what you don't have; he tends to ask for what is precious to you. For many, time is the most precious commodity. And God wants to know you will give him a portion of what is precious to you.

When you spend time in the presence of the Lord, it becomes an expression of worship which ministers to the heart of God.

As you read what is written within these pages, I want you to be open to what God is going to teach you. The concepts and practices you learn will revolutionize your meditation and prayer time, thereby enhancing your daily living. I pray that as you learn to meditate on God's Word, you will become the expressed image of Christ and obtain the good life God has prepared for you.

The scriptural premise of this book is found in Joshua 1:8: "Do not let this Book of the Law depart from your mouth; meditate on it day and night, so that you may be careful to do everything written in it. Then you will be prosperous and successful." Success is a direct benefit of meditation. Everything that exists in the world today is the result of a sustained thought—either God's or a person's—that has been birthed into the earth and is now called a reality. In essence, that is what meditation really is, a sustained thought. Let us now go on to define meditation and how it can influence our lives.

Chapter 2
The Process of Think, Say, See, and Be

Meditation is the inexpressible longing of the inner man for the infinite.

—HP Blavatsky

Listening to God's Gentle Voice

There are many aspects of prayer and meditation is one of the most effective. It may not seem at first that meditation is a form of prayer, but I promise you it is. Remember that prayer is a conversation with God, and while we're awfully good at talking with God, we're not as good at listening to him. Meditation is simply listening to the heart of God.

It may be more accurate to say that meditation is focused "not-talking." There's a story about Mother Teresa, who was interviewed by Dan Rather. Rather asked her, "What do you say when you pray?"

"I don't say anything. I listen," she responded.

Rather pressed her: "Well, then, what does God say?"

She responded, "He doesn't say anything. He listens."

So maybe, even while we're meditating on God, God's meditating on us. Meditation is thinking on God's goodness and his Word. It is actively listening for that gentle, small voice to speak to your heart. But even if he doesn't speak to you audibly, meditation is sitting quietly before God, enjoying his presence while pondering the words he has already spoken to you.

Remember the story of Elijah in the cave? It represents the power and strength of the quietness of God's presence.

> The Lord said, "Go out and stand on the mountain in the presence of the Lord, for the Lord is about to pass by." Then a great and powerful wind tore the mountains apart and shattered the rocks before the Lord, but the Lord was not in the wind. After the wind there was an earthquake, but the Lord was not in the earthquake. After the earthquake came a fire, but the Lord was not in the fire. And after the fire came a gentle whisper. When Elijah heard it, he pulled his cloak over his face and went out and stood at the mouth of the cave. (1 Kings 19:11–13)

How are we supposed to hear that gentle, still, small voice if all our life is full of strong winds, earthquakes, and fires? That's not just a rhetorical question—there's an answer to it. We only hear that gentle, still, small voice by being still and quiet, while focusing on it and nothing else. The Elijah story suggests that we cannot neglect quiet time with God because that is when he often gives us the most essential instructions for our life. It also teaches us that God has a myriad of different ways he speaks with us and we cannot limit him to our preferred styles of communication. We submit to *him* and allow *him* to be God in our lives. So begin to quiet yourself and your life, because some things you will only hear him speak during your time of meditation.

Defining Meditation

Meditation is one of those words that means different things to different people. It's an ancient discipline, older than Christianity, and practiced by almost every religion in the world, as well as by many people who aren't religious at all. It involves being still and quiet, focusing your mind on one thought, object, or image. It's not the emptying of your mind that is the focus, but directing your mind toward something, inviting it in, and giving it your attention—it is rather filling your mind. Meditation begins with our thoughts and our thought processes, eventually changing our very thinking and the paradigms we live our lives by.

The process of meditation begins with deciding what you desire for your life. Once you decide what you want your life to look like, you must then begin to feed your mind and thoughts information, images, concepts, and principles that are consistent with your desired end. The formula I want you to consider in an effort to understand the way meditation works and the benefits of meditation is this: "Think, See, Say, and Be."

Think, See, Say, and Be

If you *think* it often enough and deeply enough, you will see it through dreams, visions, images, etc. As you *see* or envision it, you will then *say* it, declare it, and decree it. Through the Spirit of God you have the power to call those things that are not as though they already are.[2] Further, Job 22:28 says, "What

---

[2]. "As it is written: 'I have made you a father of many nations.' He is our father in the sight of God, in whom he believed—the God who gives life to the dead and calls things that are not as though they were." (Romans 4:17)

you decide on will be done, and light will shine on your ways," which means whenever you speak in accordance with the Word and will of God, he will give you the wisdom, understanding, and divine strategy necessary to bring your thoughts into manifestation. Finally, after you decree what you see, you will then *be* it. You will receive the manifestation, making real in your life what was originally once a thought.

Let's look at each step of the process a little more deeply.

Think

The human mind is fascinating! It operates from two aspects of consciousness: the conscious and the subconscious mind. These two aspects work well together but their functions are very different. The conscious mind is the part of the brain that is responsible for logic and reasoning. If I asked you to distinguish a grey cat from a black dog, your conscious mind would be used to make that decision. The conscious mind also controls all the actions that you intentionally do, like moving your hands, legs, feet, etc. The conscious mind is also the security guard for the mind. If someone tried to present you with information that is against your understanding of reality, then your conscious mind will filter it and discard it.

On the other hand, if some information is presented to your conscious mind that agrees with your belief system, the conscious will transfer that information into your subconscious mind and cause your actions, decisions, words, and life to be aligned with the information that the conscious mind has deemed the truth.

The subconscious mind is running your life without you even being aware of it. But it can also be changed. The subconscious mind is where your instincts are formed, where you act without thinking about it. With enough disciplined focus on the Word of God, acting faithfully will become second nature, something you do without thinking about it. Praising God will be as natural as breathing. This is where we find the amazing power of meditating on God's Word.

God originally created us for goodness, but sin and negativity are an inseparable part of our human nature since the Fall. Therefore we must be taught the Word of God in order to correct what sin has done to our lives. As a result of our sinful state, the nature of our paradigms was also developed based on sin. A paradigm is a system of thought which affects our life's decisions. The quality of our life's decisions directly impact the quality of life we live in reality. With this understanding we must admit that if our paradigms are not changed from their original sinful nature, we will only be able to produce a life of sin and negativity.

However, if we allow the Word of God to renew our paradigms, then our conscious mind will allow positive righteous information to be accepted into our subconscious mind, thus enabling us to produce a successful life in Christ. As we build a lifestyle of meditation on God's Word, it rewires the conscious and subconscious mind and re-creates a paradigm or thought-structure that is based on the Word of God. Once the conscious mind identifies with the Word of God or receives a word from God, it then transfers that word into the subconscious mind and causes us to live a continual victorious life in Christ. God's desire is that our minds be transformed and cleansed by the Word of God.

Paul reminded the Romans: "Do not conform any longer to the pattern of this world, but be transformed by the renewing of your mind. Then you will be able to test and approve what God's will is—his good, pleasing and perfect will" (Romans 12:2).

You must start renewing your conscious mind today through the Word of God if you want anything to change in your life! It really is a mind thing. Feelings are nice, and they are a gift from God, but it's in our minds that commitment, discipline, and faith are born and sustained.

Whatever you think you will ultimately become: "For as he (a man or a woman) thinketh in his heart, so is he…" (Proverbs 23:7, KJV). The word "thinketh" implies that a person continues to reflect on and sustain thoughts on specific information, images, concepts, or principles. Those thoughts eventually bear fruit in their character and choices, thus affecting who they are at the core of their being.

Whatever you put in your mind determines what comes out in your words and deeds. In Philippians 4:8 the apostle Paul encourages us to program our minds with thoughts that are true, noble, right, pure, lovely, and admirable. Consistently thinking these thoughts builds a wall of protection around our life that is difficult for the enemy to penetrate.

See

The next phase of this important process is the *see* or *envision* component of the formula. This is where your sustained thoughts begin to create mental images, dreams, or visions. As you proceed to the destination God has planned for you, it is important for you to have a mental picture of your future state.

Helen Keller, an educator who was deaf and blind, was asked a critical question: "What is worse than being blind?" She responded, "The only thing worse than being blind is having sight but no vision." This statement is powerful and gives credence and support to the school of thought that says if you can see the invisible you can do the impossible. Your ability to see or envision your future is a major determining factor in whether or not you will receive your future expectation.

Whatever you allow to remain in your thought life will ultimately influence your words and deeds. Proverbs 29:18 says, "Where there is no vision, the people perish; but he that keepeth the law, happy is he." (KJV) "Vision" in this passage is *hazon*, which means "revelation" or a revealing of God's original plan for your life or situation. The Word of God unveils His plans for you and gives you the ability to see clearly what is accessible to you. Ultimately, true success can only be seen through the binoculars of God's Word. Therefore, your ability to see or envision your successful future hinges on the revelation of His Word.

It's also true that the more time you spend studying something, the more it will influence the way you see everything around you. If you study nutrition, for example, you'll find that the more you know about preservatives, the more you see them and their effects in everything your family eats. You'll spend huge amounts of time and energy seeing good and bad nutrition wherever you are, and seeing the good and bad outcomes of nutritional choices for the people you love—and that's because your thoughts have influenced what you see. Before you started studying nutrition, you never saw it or thought about what it meant for your family's future.

This is how our minds work. The more time we spend thinking about something, the more we see it, understand it, and the more clearly we can envision what it will mean for us. It works exactly the same way as we meditate on the Word of God.

Say

Your words are powerful beyond comprehension. Your tongue has the ability to create or destroy, to build up or demolish, and to bless or curse. Proverbs 18:21 says, "The tongue has the power of life and death, and those who love it will eat its fruit." "Eat its fruit" means that however you choose to use your tongue will determine the kind of life you will live.

If you speak positive things then you will obtain positive fruit, and likewise, if you are always speaking negatively, negativity will be your harvest. God made you a speaking spirit and gave you dominion over the earth and everything therein. One of the main benefits to being a speaking spirit is that you have the ability to create the world you want by the words of your mouth.

It isn't always clear how we create our own world through the words we use, but it's a power received from God by being made in his image. God speaks, and worlds are created—likewise, we speak in the power of God and worlds are created. They are smaller, more intimate worlds; but for good or ill, they are our worlds.

> We can see how God did this, and continually does this, in the first chapter of Genesis:
>
> And God said, "Let there be light," and there was light. (Genesis 1:3)
>
> And God said, "Let there be an expanse between the waters to separate water from water.... And it was so." (Genesis 1:6–7)
>
> And God said, "Let the water under the sky be gathered to one place, and let dry ground appear." And it was so. (Genesis 1:9)
>
> Then God said, "Let the land produce vegetation: seed-bearing plants and trees on the land that bear fruit with seed in it, according to their various kinds." And it was so. (Genesis 1:11)
>
> And God said, "Let there be lights in the expanse of the sky to separate the day from the night, and let them serve as signs to mark seasons, and days and years…" (Genesis 1:14)
>
> And God said, "Let the water teem with living creatures, and let birds fly above the earth across the expanse of the sky." (Genesis 1:20)
>
> And God said, "Let the land produce living creatures according to their kinds: the livestock, the creatures that move along the ground, and the wild animals, each according to its kind." And it was so. (Genesis 1:24)

We see in the first chapter of Genesis where God spoke seven times saying, "Let there be," and it became whatever he commanded. Through the power of his word he created the heavens, the earth, and everything therein with the exception of man. God had a greater plan for mankind. He wanted him to be his representation in the realm of the earth.

> Then God said, "Let us make mankind in our image, in our likeness, and let them rule over the fish of the sea and the birds of the air, over the livestock, and all the earth, and over all the creatures that move along the ground." (Genesis 1:26)

Man was made in the image and likeness of God, and he was given dominion over all the earth. "The Lord God formed the man from the dust of the ground and breathed into his nostrils the breath of life, and the man became a living being" (Genesis 2:7). The Hebrew translation for "living being" is "speaking spirit." So the Hebrew translation of this verse would read, "and man became a speaking spirit."

Since we are created in the image and likeness of God, through his Spirit we can do what he did. He created the world with the words of his mouth. Likewise, God expects us to create our own world with the words of our mouth. The same Spirit of God who said, "Let there be light" in Genesis 1:3 is alive in you today. You must begin to make your "Let there be" declarations over your own life based on your desired future state.

Paul declared, "And if the Spirit of him who raised Jesus from the dead is living in you, he who raised Christ from the dead will also give life to your mortal bodies through his Spirit, who lives in you" (Romans 8:11).

You are a speaking spirit! Start using the power God gave you through the life of your tongue.

Be

It is the perfect will of God for you to live abundantly in every area of your life. The *be* portion of this formula is the manifestation of what you think, envision, and talk about. It is the place where God finally brings into manifestation the great things he has placed within your heart.

The journey to finally live the life the Word of God says you can live is not an easy one. It is filled with numerous faith fights, sacrifices, and ridicule. Many times you will feel like you are all alone and that no one truly understands what you are going through. When you feel that way always remember that God is just a call away. For Hebrews 4:15–16 says,

> For we do not have a high priest who is unable to sympathize with our weaknesses, but we have one who has been tempted in every way, just as we are—yet was without sin.

> Let us then approach God's throne of grace with confidence, so that we may receive mercy and find grace to help us in our time of need.

You must hold fast to this scripture on your journey, meditating on it deeply, because the enemy is going to do everything he can to convince you that the long process to the manifestation of God's promises is not worth it. Satan wants to convince you that waiting on God's promise is too painful, that God is taking too long to bless you, and that maybe his promises are fulfilled for everybody else but you. Satan wants you to believe his lies, because if he can change your mind he can change your destiny. Don't allow the enemy to deceive you into moving outside God's will. Hold fast! Don't let go of the promises he has made to you, for they shall surely manifest. "God is not human, that he should lie, not a human being, that he should change his mind. Does he speak and then not act? Does he promise and not fulfill? (Numbers 23:19).

But we know Satan is a liar. We will see the manifestation of God in an abundant and supernatural way. The way to begin seeing God's promises manifested is to envision them while meditating on the word of God. Remember, it was the word of God that created worlds, and through meditation, you can create the world you want as well. Or rather, he can create in you the world he wants for you.

Biblical Example of the Think, See, Say, and Be Process

The best biblical example of the "Think, See, Say, and Be" process is Joseph, the son of Jacob. Joseph is by far one of my favorite biblical characters because he exemplifies a tremendous amount of courage, integrity, grace, and resilience during his journey to greatness. He was the youngest of the eleven sons of Jacob, who was also called Israel. There was no secret that Joseph was his favorite. He was favored because he was the son of Israel's old age, and he was the first child by Rachel, his favorite wife.

Genesis 37:3 says, "Now Israel loved Joseph more than any of his other sons, because he had been born to him in his old age; and he made a richly ornamented robe for him."

The love and favor Jacob showed for Joseph provoked the other sons to jealousy. They hated Joseph. The coat of many colors represented the love, favor, approval, and support Jacob had for Joseph but not necessarily for the other sons. But the coat was not the only reason they hated him. They also hated him for his dreams — or rather, what his dreams foretold.

> Joseph had a dream, and when he told it to his brothers, they hated him all the more. He said to them, "Listen to this dream I had: We were binding sheaves of grain out in the field when suddenly my sheaf rose and stood upright, while your sheaves gathered around mine and bowed down to it."
>
> His brothers said to him, "Do you intend to reign over us? Will you actually rule us?" And they hated him all the more because of his dream and what he had said.
>
> Then he had another dream, and he told it to his brothers. "Listen," he said, "I had another dream, and this time the sun and moon and eleven stars were bowing down to me."
>
> When he told his father as well as his brothers, his father rebuked him and said, "What is this dream you had? Will your mother and I and your brothers actually come and bow down to the ground before you?" His brothers were jealous of him, but his father kept the matter in mind. (Genesis 37:5–11)

This text reveals the naivety of Joseph as he did not consider the meanings or the seriousness of his dreams; nor did he realize the negative effect his dreams would have on his brothers. Nevertheless, Joseph's ability to declare what he saw in his dreams started a chain of events, years ahead of time, that would eventually lead to the manifestation of what he had dreamed.

Often God will give you a glimpse of your destiny which is filled with so much greatness and grandeur that you will have difficulty believing he is actually talking about you. When God speaks to you, whether through dreams, visions, or prophecy, he always speaks in terms of the destiny and purpose he has predetermined for your life. God is not intimidated by where you are right now because he knows where you are headed. It is good to be reminded of what God says through Jeremiah again: "'For I know the plans I have for you,' declares the Lord, 'plans to prosper you and not to harm you, plans to give you hope and a future'" (Jeremiah 29:11).

The Pain and Pressure of the Process

While the picture of your future looks wonderful, no one can really prepare you for the pain and pressure you will encounter in the process of getting to your destination. The power to be sustained through the pain and pressure of the process comes exclusively from the Word and the Spirit of God. If you are not careful to become securely planted in the Word of God, you will praise over the prophecy, and later abort the process by immaturity. Because the process can seem to be so contrary to the prophecy, you will mistake the process by calling it persecution, eventually quitting. By quitting you forfeit everything God has shown you and you are reduced to living a limited life. But if you allow the Word to be a lamp unto your feet and a light unto your path, you will not be deceived into quitting, but endure so you will receive the manifested promises God has for you. David said, "I am still confident of this: I will see the goodness of the Lord in the land of the living" (Psalm 27:13).

I'm sure Joseph had some inkling that he was headed for prominence, but I don't think he would have readily embraced it if someone would told him, "Now God has a great life planned for you. But in order for you to get there you will be hated by your brothers. They will hate you so much until they will want to kill you, but God will intervene and they will just throw you in a pit with no water for a while, and then sell you to some merchant men who will auction you off to the highest bidder as if you were an antique grandfather clock. Ah…but don't worry, the Lord is with you…"

That was Joseph's process, but you have your own process to endure. Nevertheless, the story of Joseph is a great example of what God will do for you if you remain faithful to him to by trusting his Word. Every great man or woman of God has a process to endure and, the truth is, our flesh does not want to suffer. But God promises that if we suffer with him, we will also reign with him.

Jesus is our ultimate example, and in the Garden of Gethsemane we get a glimpse of his humanity not wanting to endure the process. On the way to the cross, Jesus stopped by the Garden of Gethsemane to pray. He said to God, "If it be your will, let this cup pass from me." Like us, he didn't want to suffer, but was finally able to trust his Father completely: "yet not my will, but yours be done" (Luke 22:42).

Chapter 3
Meditation's Attributes and Benefits

Meditation in Action

Joseph meditated on the revelation, the word of God he received, and eventually that word created a new world for him. Even Jacob, his father, meditated on what Joseph had dreamed about. But what is meditation and how does it work in the life of a believer? Meditation is not being mindless and staring aimlessly into space; but it is the process of controlling your thoughts and being empowered by them.

You could say that meditation is focused silence. It's a silence you choose, and in our crowded lives, silence is like a much needed space in our heads, hearts, and lives. So we grab that space, claim it for our own, and push everything else out of it. For the moment, in this space, it's only us, all by ourselves, alone.

Being alone is not a bad thing in and of itself. How often are we really alone, with no noise, demands, or worries pressing on us from every direction? Not very often. As the poet Jean Arp puts it, "Soon silence will have passed into legend. Man has turned his back on silence. Day after day he invents machines and devices that increase noise and distract humanity from the essence of life, contemplation, meditation." Even when no other people are around, the car radio is on, the television is on, or our minds are being crowded by the flood of words pouring into them from the computer, iPod, or the screen of our cell phones.

Sacred Space

These words, the constant activity and noise, are perceived as a continual threat—as a battle—by our harried minds and bodies. And in a very natural response our body kicks into battle gear. Blood sugar spikes, cortisol (the stress hormone) increases, adrenaline rushes, blood pressure elevates, and our bodies respond like they're under attack all the time. That's what we call stress.

Nobody can live like that—not well at least, or long. The first thing to get your body and mind out of battle mode is to turn off the battle noise. Turn off the television, radio, phone, and computer; grab some space. If all you do in this space is stop fighting for a few minutes, it would be well worth it in and of itself. Of course, that's not all you're going to do; but we'll get to that in a minute.

Space can be hard to find, but the truth is that if it matters to you, you'll find it. There's no point making any excuses about how busy you are—all God's children are busy. Joseph was busy, but he was able to hear and meditate on a dream from God. Jacob was busy, but he was able to raise thirteen kids and consider how God was working in their lives. We're all busy in the daily routine of our lives, but it is possible to find this space.

When you start to think about how busy you are and how you could never find the time to sit in silence, even for only a few minutes, I want you to think of Susanna Wesley. Susanna was a preacher's wife and mother of ten kids. She homeschooled all those kids, and when her husband was gone—which was often—she ran his church for him and took care of his people. She was the Sunday school director and made sure everyone, adults and kids alike, received good biblical instruction in the faith. She wrote letters, called on the sick, cooked, cleaned, mended, and studied, keeping those ten kids in line every day, without a lot of help from her husband.

Every day, without fail, Susanna found an entire hour to meditate. Where was she supposed to go with ten kids and half the church over at her house? She went inside her head. She sat in a kitchen chair and pulled her apron up over her face; and everyone knew that when Mama had her apron up, she was spending her quiet time with Jesus, and you didn't bother her. The noise went on around her, but she stepped out of the battle to spend an hour in focused silence.

It is possible to step out of the battle that we fight every day and find quiet time with Jesus. And if that is all we did, it would be good for us. But after we push everything and everyone out of that quiet space, we're going to let one thing back in—or maybe one person. For some, being alone with God may be frightening because it forces you to hear yourself think and face what's really in your head. Most people are so preoccupied with life and its challenges that they have lost touch with God and themselves. Daily meditating on God will help you center yourself, reconnect with God, and develop a more effective and productive way of living. After we shove out all of the words, we're going to just pick one or two words to let back in...and when we do that, we let the Word in.

Focused Silence

Meditation is focused silence. And in Christian meditation, what we're focusing on is the Word of God. Now the Word of God is Jesus, like it says in the gospel of John:

> In the beginning was the Word, and the Word was with God, and the Word was God. He was with God in the beginning. Through him all things were made; without him nothing was made that has been made.... The Word became flesh and made his dwelling among us. We have seen his glory, the glory of the One and Only, who came from the Father, full of grace and truth. (John 1:1–3, 14)

Jesus, the Word of God, comes to us in his words, especially those found in the Bible. If we make some room, the Holy Spirit opens a door, and those words from God come right in, bringing the one true Word of God with them.

Meditation is being quiet in the presence of those words, but being quiet for a reason. The reason is to invite a friend in to spend some time with him. In that time you have together, the time that's just for the two of you and nobody else, he'll teach you things, he'll comfort you and strengthen you and encourage you, and he'll show you more love than you've ever known before. How could you have time for this? When you're in the battle, you can't stop fighting for survival. There's no time or energy to enjoy the affection of a friend. But when you step off the battlefield, you start to notice peace, beauty, and love.

A Form of Prayer

For Christians, meditation is a form of prayer. We have a long history of brothers and sisters who met God deep inside the quiet space. We're going to look at some of that later — from the biblical call to meditation to the contemporary movements toward silent prayer, centering prayer, and contemplation — which are all ways of referring to Christian meditation.

Someone once said, "Prayer is you talking to God. Meditation is God talking to you." Many believers pray what I call "drive-by prayers." They drive by, drop off their demands and requests, and expect it to be delivered on the exact day and time requested. Think about that for a moment. From the time we're kids, we're taught to pray *for* things. "Tell God this, ask God that. Tell

God that someone hurt your feelings today. Tell God that you're worried about Grandma, and ask him to make her healthy again." Don't get me wrong, those are great ways to pray because God loves us and wants to hear our thoughts and feelings. God is ready to give if only we'll ask. And God is ready to listen if only we'll confide in him.

But that's only a one-way conversation. Think about your relationship with someone you love—your husband or wife, your child or best friend. What if they talked about their life all the time, asking you for help and guidance, but was never quiet long enough to let you offer the help they needed? What if they knew you could give them some advice that would make them feel better, but they never stopped talking long enough to hear what you had to say? You'd be frustrated, right? You'd be exasperated because you would know you could help them, if only they'd be quiet long enough to listen.

That's how God feels sometimes. You want a word from God, don't you? You know he has wisdom and strength and peace and encouragement and love to offer you. How is he supposed to get those into your mind and heart if they never sit still long enough for the Holy Spirit to get the door open?

Meditation is sitting still long enough for the Holy Spirit to get the door open and deliver a word from God. It is a reciprocal two-way conversation, from us to God, and from God back to us again. He comes to us and listens so patiently, like a gentle Father, but he wants to be heard too. He loves us and he wants to spend time with us. Just as we desire to feel valued and treasured, he has the same feelings. After all, we were created in his image and likeness. Meditation is spending quality time with the Father, during which he gives us wisdom, strength, peace, and whatever else we may need.

In other words, what God gives you during your time of meditation are the gifts you cannot obtain alone. Righteousness, peace, and joy can only be given by the Father; and it is through these divine elements that prosperity and increase emanate. God does not want us to miss the blessings he has in store for us; but we must keep all things in proper perspective. Many believers spend their "prayer time" seeking the hand of God (stuff, material things, husband, wife, etc.) instead of the heart of God (love, righteousness, peace, and joy). This is, as my mother would say, putting the cart before the horse. But it's out of order!

Jesus said, "Your heavenly Father knows that you need them. But seek first his kingdom and his righteousness, and all these things will be given to you as well" (Matthew 6:32–33). Meditating on the Word of God is the act of putting the kingdom of God first. Once you put God first he promises to add all *things* to your life. If you desire to put God first, pray this prayer and receive the empowerment to make him first in your life today:

Father, in the name of Jesus, I repent before you now for allowing anything or anyone to be first in my life but you. Please forgive me and wash my mind, heart, and spirit from anything that is not like you.

Today I ask you to bring my spirit into alignment with your Spirit. Help me to honor and acknowledge you in all my ways so that my thoughts will be established according to your Word.

I desire to seek first your kingdom and righteousness. I renounce idolatry, materialism, a haughty spirit, the pride of life, the love of money, addictions, backsliding, prayerlessness, carnality, fear, and any other demonic spirits that have operated in my life.

I declare and decree that today my spiritual ears are open and my heart is submitted to your perfect plan for me. Today I pull off carnality and I put on righteousness, peace, and joy in the Holy Ghost, in the name of Jesus. Amen.

Meditation's Benefits

Not everyone who meditates is seeking a deeper relationship with God; and a deeper prayer life isn't the only benefit to meditating. There are almost endless benefits to meditation, from better relationships to improved health, which is why so many people through the ages have considered it important.

One of the most significant benefits of meditating on the Word of God is that it has a unique ability to show you who you really are, in regards to how you think, act, and feel. Many believers are secretly afraid to be quiet with God because they are forced to hear their thoughts and deal with their feelings. For many it is difficult to face who they really are. Therefore they crowd their lives with activities, hobbies, people they don't even like, phone calls, Internet surfing, and when all else fails they listen to the radio even while they sleep. For some it's been years since they have visited with themselves and heard their own thoughts. One of the first things God's Word does is take on the characteristics of a mirror, showing you who you really are, who you should be, and who you will become.

In this sense, the benefits of meditation are not only spiritual, but also natural. Research shows that people who meditate are calmer, more thoughtful, less anxious, healthier, and more patient people than those who do not meditate. The Word of God enables you to live the abundant life God promised you.

Meditation can also be a form of healing — just one more way in which God brings his healing power to our lives. Our busyness, battle-fighting, noise, and activity serve to cover over our hurts, sins, and fears. When those fester within, our hearts get infected and infect other parts of our lives without being aware of it. But if we strip those coverings away, even for just a few minutes, those wounds can then rise to the surface, where light can shine on them, thus bringing healing. We learn in those moments of meditation what's really inside of us, and we offer it up to be blessed or healed.

Meditation is going to change you for the better. Even non-Christians are changed by meditation, becoming calmer, more thoughtful, less anxious, healthier, patienter, and having the sense that there is space inside their heads and hearts, where they can find enjoyment, laughter, and peace.

While meditation brings peace inside your head and your heart, it's not just a mental thing. Meditation is something you do with your entirety — body, mind, and spirit. It's a kind of prayer that involves your breath, your heartbeat, your hands, legs, and back. When you are calm and you've made room for peace, your heart rate goes down while your oxygen level increases. When you meditate, you breathe deeply and rhythmically, and your thinking becomes clearer (all that oxygen getting to your brain cells helps), your anxiety levels go down, and even the knots in your muscles start to untie themselves. As one doctor put it, "Any condition that's caused or worsened by stress can be alleviated through meditation."

Another great thing about meditation is that it can be started anytime and can be done almost anywhere. You don't need any special training or skills, and you don't have to have half the Bible memorized to begin. Meditation is a gift that's given to lifelong Christians and beginners alike. If you can breathe and know the name of Jesus, that's all you need to get started. This is consistent with the way God treats us in every area — sure, he wants us to advance, to be stronger and to go deeper, but mostly he wants us to be with him now, and he'll honor our efforts to do just that.

Meditation Prepares the Heart

Remember when we said earlier that some people think they're too busy to meditate? It's true that people are busy doing many valuable things, but when the good things you are doing start to hinder your ability to spend time with God, you must stop and reassess the value of what you're doing. That assessment can be accomplished by asking yourself a few questions. Is what I'm doing a *good* thing, or is it a *God* thing? Who am I trying to please with what I'm doing? Did God tell me to do this or have I just gotten caught up doing it and now feel obligated to keep doing it? If God told me to start doing this, could he now be telling me to stop doing it? Your truthful answer to these questions will determine when and how you should restructure your life to make time for God.

Many believers have just become victims of the ADHD (Attention Deficit Hyperactive Disorder) environment that we live in. Everything is always moving but very little is being accomplished. My mother use to call it "going nowhere fast." We have lost focus, creativity, energy, and alertness. We major in the minors by giving too much of our time to petty issues. We spend too much time on the Internet, Facebook, and Twitter as we voyeuristically keep up with everybody's life while losing our own.

If this sounds like you, stop now, and make the decision to slow down and readjust your behavior so you can hear God speak to you on a daily basis, because right now you are "going nowhere fast."

Perhaps you are like me—multigifted in the things of God and a person of many passions. There was a time in my life when I was so busy with the work of the Lord I didn't have time to pray. When I did have time I didn't have the energy. I was preaching, teaching, singing, choir directing, planning conferences and revivals. I was doing the work of the Lord—or so I thought. One day the Lord spoke to me and said, "Yes, you are busy with my work, but your relationship with me is suffering. Don't get so busy with the work of the Lord that you forget the Lord of work. Ministry work is no substitute for prayer and meditation. When you get in a spiritual rut, a choir rehearsal can't get you out of it. You need a word from me."

If you can relate to any of this, I challenge you to make your relationship with God your top priority and everything else will fall into place.

The most important thing to remember about meditation is that it has to be done consistently. It's like exercise: sometimes we get inspired and we go out and jog three miles, but then we come home and don't exercise again for a year. That is not going to get us in shape! Instead of doing a lot on one day and nothing later, it's better to do a little every day. The habit, discipline, or commitment of meditating is as important as what you do in your actual meditation sessions. This is true in part because meditation not only *opens* the heart to receive a word from God, it also *prepares* the heart to take in that word when it comes.

A preacher I know tells the story of her mother, growing up in the Depression. The family had an old second-hand piano, and the girl loved to play; but once the Depression came, there was no money to repair the piano and it eventually fell silent. It didn't matter to the girl though. She sat down at that bench every day and practiced, running her fingers up and down silent keys, making no music at all. One day her mother asked her, "Why do you bother to do this every day? It's a waste of time!" The girl replied, "I want to be ready when the music comes."

The girl continued to do this for several years, getting exasperated looks from family members every time. And then, one day, a note played. A single key played its music. And for weeks that was all. But then another note played, until, after several months, the piano's music was restored, key by key. And the girl was there, ready for it, able to make the piano sing because she had shown up day after day, even when it looked like wasted time to everyone else.

Meditation is the act of returning to that spiritual piano bench day in and day out; it is the work of playing scales and hymns when it feels like nobody can hear them. Meditation is getting the heart ready for the music of God to pour into it.

So how do you begin? We're going to look at several different ways to meditate in a later chapter, ways that depend on how your mind works and how you relax and listen. But some of the basics are the same for everybody. And those we will discuss now.

Chapter 4
The Reasons and Practicalities of Meditation

Your Internal Conversation

Why don't more people meditate? That is a question I often think about myself. I think the reason why more people don't meditate can be as varied as the amount of people there are in the world. Nevertheless, I think that deep down many have bought into the idea that meditating is "doing nothing," and we feel guilty about doing nothing when there are so many things that need to be done. Most of what needs to be done are good things, many of them are even godly things. Many Christians are busy at the church—leading Bible studies, cleaning the worship space, preparing Sunday school classes, organizing food drives, or creating and distributing ministry media. Those Christians are busy for the love of God and out of a desire to see his kingdom grow. They have a lot to do, the kingdom isn't going to grow by itself, and they don't have time to just sit still and do nothing.

If you're one of those busy servant-Christians, you have to change the conversation that goes on inside your head. If you are so busy loving and serving the church, doing your job, or taking care of your family that you have no time to meditate, there are some things I want you to keep in mind.

The Only Place You can't be Replaced is in Your Relationships

What if you didn't fold the newsletter or mow the church's lawn? Who would do it? The answer is someone. *Someone* would do it. But do you want to stand before God's throne on Judgment Day and try to explain to him that you never had time to listen to him because you were too busy cleaning his house or folding his newsletters? Think about this in human terms—you wouldn't neglect your spouse or kids just to do some important chore, would you? If your daughter or son needed you to listen, you'd stop your housework and listen, right? The dishes will eventually get done—but your child is more important. It's the same way with God. The work around the church, office, or house will eventually get done, but right now God is asking you to stop and listen to him.

A Prayerful Person is the Best Evangelist

The work and ministry that go on in the church matter immensely. It's important that we have good music, clean classrooms, and useful Sunday school lessons. But what gets people into the church to enjoy those things in the first place? It's always a connection with someone they know. The conversion process starts because someone met someone and thought, "He seems so centered, so peaceful. I wish I could be like that." Or maybe it was, "Even when things are bad, she just seems so joyful. How does she do that?" They realize they do it through spending quiet time with Jesus on a consistent basis, and Jesus uses that to draw others to himself. Can you be that person for someone?

Meditation Isn't "Doing Nothing"

Is a sunset walk holding hands with your boyfriend or girlfriend "doing nothing?" Is humming softly to a baby as you rock him to sleep "doing nothing?" Is holding a phone to your ear for two hours while a friend works out a problem "doing nothing?" Is pacing the hospital waiting room while your parent is in surgery "doing nothing?" Of course not. These are the moments when relationships are made and strengthened. These are the moments when you're reminded of what really matters in life, and what you would lose if it were gone. These are the moments when all that matters is the other person and the love between you two. That's what meditation is. That's what you're "doing" when you sit in focused silence with the Lord.

It's hard to change this mindset when we're used to "doing," and used to showing someone how much we value them by what we do for them. When it comes to God and our other relationships in our lives we need to get our minds around less "doing," and more "being." Just be together for a while, with no guilt and no pressure and no worries about what's being left undone. You have permission from God; now it's time to give yourself the same permission.

Why Do People Meditate?

People who have never thought of themselves as the meditating type often find that at some point in their lives they are drawn to it. There are many reasons to start meditating, and these reasons can be physical, emotional, or spiritual. For example, meditation helps with heart disease, diabetes, depression, anger, anxiety, and high blood pressure—and I know those things matter a lot.

We'll spend the whole third section of the book talking about just how good meditation can be in every part of a person's life.

But right now we're focusing on Christian meditation, which is different from a simple health-based meditation, and even different from the meditation practiced in other religions. Christian meditation establishes or reinforces the believer's love-walk with Christ. To learn the Word of God and commit to aligning your life with his Word becomes an expression of your love for him. He says in John 14:14–15, "You may ask me for anything in my name, and I will do it. If you love me, you will obey what I command." As you embrace the Word of God, you embrace his precepts, laws, commandments, and the essence of who he is. In this you strengthen your relationship with Christ. God is love and God is the Word. As you increase in the Word you increase in love. They cannot be separated.

Every aspect of the Christian life, and that includes meditation, has two purposes: to declare that Jesus is Lord and to draw the believer closer to God.

For us as believers, it can be enough to know that God is God and Jesus is Lord. Because we know these are true, the right reaction is to proclaim Jesus' lordship and do everything we can to get closer to God. In a sense, it doesn't matter how we feel about it, because we know we're supposed to be obedient to God, and that's enough. But God, being a generous and caring Father, has made us so that we get more than just being obedient out of our relationship with him.

While we should have a desire to be obedient to God, there's something deep inside every human being that wants more than that. We want to know and be known in the depths of our souls. We want to love and be loved by someone who sees all the dark corners and sinful places in our hearts and still wraps us in a warm embrace. We want to be part of something bigger than our own small lives, connected to things that matter. We want to be taken care of, and we want to be depended on. Human beings in some ways are nothing but a big ache for love, because that's how God made us.

And while others may love us and ease the ache a little, only God can truly satisfy our need for love. This is because, deep down, it's his love we need the most. Sometimes people start to feel that need and realize it has always been there, even if they're just now able to identify it. There's always been something inside each of us that cries out to be close to God. When we finally hear that cry, many people turn to Christian meditation as a way to get the closeness they want so badly.

Let me give you an example. In 2003 God shifted my entire life into a zone that I was not expecting. The year prior, God began to instruct me to give things away. I have always been proud to call myself a giver but he was challenging me in ways I had never before been challenged. I would buy a new suit and bring it home with plans to wear it and God would tell me to give it away. Nice pieces of jewelry, two cars—on separate occasions he told me to give them away.

At the time I didn't understand why God would have me to give away things that were so personal and important to me. I now realize it was all preparation for the day he would tell me to leave everything I ever knew and loved and move to a place where I only knew a few people to start a church. I left my mother and family who I loved very much. I left my then fiancé, who is now my loving wife. I left my pastor and church family with whom I had served for more than twenty years. When I landed in Portland, Oregon, in October of 2003, I had five dollars to my name, a cell phone, two suitcases of clothing, and a word from God. I've been a believer most of my life, but it was time for me to experience God in a greater way.

Nothing was familiar. Everything had changed except the voice of God. Although I had been saved for about twenty years at that point and was very familiar with the voice of God, I literally lived by every word that proceeded out of the mouth of God each day. I could not afford to miss a day from hearing God's voice.

I felt alone, fought depression daily for more than a year, and many of my friendships were terminated. My best friend was killed in a car accident a month after I moved. I felt like everything I counted on was being stripped away. I was stranded in the will of God with no place to run but to his Word. I felt like Elisha in 1 Kings 19. When Elijah found Elisha plowing in his father's field, he walked past him and cast a mantle over him that would shift his life forever. Elijah was getting ready to leave, but that mantle activated something in Elisha that caused him to realize it was time for him to leave what he was comfortable with and follow the will of God for his life. As Elijah started to leave, Elisha said, "Please, sir, wait. I must follow you." Elisha stopped plowing and ran in the house to kiss his mother and father goodbye. On his way back out, he ran past the ox with which he had just finished plowing. He stopped, killed, and cooked the ox, fed it to his workers, and followed after Elijah.

There were two profound things God spoke to me as I read this portion of Scripture.

1) The way to greatness is through servanthood. God will only elevate you from a place of service. You must be spiritually alert and able to discern when a season has ended and allow God to begin a new era in your life.

2) When you decide to follow God, you will have to kiss some things goodbye and kill some things. Elisha kissed his parents because it was important that they knew he loved them but that he had to follow God. He killed the ox (representing his job) so that as he followed the man of God and things became difficult he would not be able to go back to his old job. He knew that it was more profitable to be stranded in the will of God than to abort his destiny, going back to a life that no longer existed for him.

Everything in me wanted to run back to Mississippi, but I'm not the turn-around type. So I stuck it out and it was during this rough transitional period in my life and ministry that I learned the value of meditation and prayer. I began to get out of bed every morning at five o'clock to meditate and pray. The first scripture I meditated on was Psalm 91.

> He that dwelleth in the secret place of the most High shall abide under the shadow of the Almighty. I will say of the Lord, He is my refuge and my fortress: my God; in him will I trust. Surely he shall deliver thee from the snare of the fowler, and from the noisome pestilence. He shall cover thee with his feathers, and under his wings shalt thou trust: his truth shall be thy shield and buckler. Thou shalt not be afraid for the terror by night, nor for the arrow that flieth by day; Nor for the pestilence that walketh in darkness; nor for the destruction that wasteth at noonday. A thousand shall fall at thy side, and ten thousand at thy right hand; but it shall not come nigh thee. Only with thine eyes shalt thou behold and see the reward of the wicked. Psalms 91: 1-8 (KJV)

God assured me through this Word that he was with me and that I was hidden in his presence from my enemy. And because of his Word my life has never been the same. I know you have your own challenges right now, but use them as motivation to get closer to God and his presence will change your life forever.

People come to God in meditation for their own reasons, but at the root of all those reasons is a desire to do what we were created to do—to be close to God. Their mouths might say, "I need some peace," or "I'm so lonely," or "I'm sorry," but their hearts are saying, "Lord, I'm restless until I rest in you."

A Time and a Place

If your heart is telling you that it wants to be closer to God, there's nothing left to do but begin. Anyone can meditate—*anyone*.

First, you need to find a time and a place to meditate. It doesn't have to be a long amount of time, especially at first; some people suggest you can begin with as little as five minutes. One book even says that three minutes of meditation is a good start. Once you get going, you'll want more time, but for now three to five minutes is a great way to begin. Get a timer; a kitchen timer is fine, or most cell phones have alarms on them as well. That way you don't have to keep peeking at the clock during this time. When can you find three to five minutes of quiet in your day?

Think about this a little creatively for a moment. If you work an eight-hour shift, you're supposed to get a thirty-minute meal break and two fifteen-minute breaks. You can sit at your desk like Susanna Wesley and close your eyes for a few minutes during one of those breaks. Later we'll learn how repetitive actions can be meditative, but for now try to find just a few minutes when you don't have to do anything else. Try to avoid meditating late at night or when you're sleepy, or right before or after meals when your energy tends to drop.

Now that you know when to meditate, begin to think about where. In a living room chair? On the edge of your bed? In the break room? How about your car when you get to work but before you go into the building? The place you meditate should be comfortable, but not so comfortable it puts you to sleep! You should be able to sit with your feet flat on the floor and your back straight.

Obviously these are ideals, and maybe you can't find a time or place quite this perfect. Just do your best to find a place and a few minutes to use it. God desires your presence, so remember, quality over quantity. He would rather meet you every day for five minutes than one hour once a week. Consistency is paramount.

Ask God to show you a good time and place for meditation, and lots of good ideas will come to you.

Practice

There is an easy way to teach yourself to meditate, especially if you're a beginner. At this point you're just practicing, but you should start with a prayer. Let God know you're starting this because you want to hear from him and draw closer to him. Let him know you're aware it's going to be difficult, but you're willing to try. You could say something like this:

Father, you have taught us that to become one with your Word is to be one with you. So today I make the commitment to sit down for three to five minutes to meditate on your Word and your goodness. Although I am new to this, I ask that your Spirit would lead and guide me. Father, as I enter into your presence, help me to close out all the distractions of life and concentrate on you only. Empower me to become consistent and passionate about my time with you every day. Thank you for accepting me as your beloved and empowering me to prosper through your Word. In the name of Jesus, I pray. Amen!

Now you've asked God to bless your trying, sit in your quiet place during your three-to-five minute time slot. Get comfortable. Now, breathe slowly and deeply, inhaling through your nose and exhaling out your mouth. Count as you breathe in (one), out (two), in (three), out (four), all the way up to ten. Don't think about anything but your breath and the numbers you're saying. Close your eyes if the things around you distract you.

Once you've mastered these two skills—breathing and counting—you're ready to meditate. You'll move on from there to deeper, Christ-centered meditation, of course, and sometimes you'll have the Bible open in front of you, but the principle will be the same: breathe deeply and focus on the word or words you've chosen to meditate on.

The rest of this book will teach you how to make your meditation Christ-centered and to build a discipline of meditation on the Word of God every day. There are many ways to meditate, but the most important thing is that you return to God in his Word with an open mind and open heart every day. Meditation is prayer, and prayer is a two-way conversation with God. For believers it's a way to obey a command from God and to draw closer to him and live a successful life every day.

Chapter 5

The Biblical Mandate

Meditation Throughout the Old Testament

The first book of the Bible is Genesis, which means beginnings. How did everything begin? It began with a word from God, and it began with the Word of God. The Hebrew language the Old Testament writers used doesn't carry over to English very well. When the English translates Genesis 1:3 as, "Let there be light," the Hebrew is more like a single word, "Light!" And when God says *a* word, what happens? That word happens. "Light." Everything that exists in heaven, earth, and underneath the earth has to obey what is decreed from God's mouth.

The same word that created the worlds is the very same word God wants to write on our hearts. He says so in Jeremiah 31:33: "I will put my law in their minds, and write it on their hearts. I will be their God, and they will be my people." How do we get that creative word in our hearts? Through meditation. How do we get that seed of creation, the creation of good things, deep in our lives? Through meditation on God's Word.

A few hundred years after God created the world and the Hebrew people, they were taken into Egyptian slavery. He sent Moses to be a bearer of his word of hope, freedom, and deliverance. Moses spoke the words of God, in the form of words of power, songs of praise, and binding commandments. Moses met face to face in his tent with the Word of God himself, listening, learning, and receiving the strength he needed. He held God's words so close to his heart and meditated on them so deeply that his life was completely changed, and everything he did glowed with the light of God.

After Moses died, his successor Joshua led the people across the Jordan and into the Promised Land. Moses had left Joshua the tablets of the law and the written record of his conversations with God, as well as God's acts of power on behalf of his people. As they stood on the river bank, preparing to claim the promise, God gave them a word of caution.

> Be strong and very courageous. Be careful to obey all the law my servant Moses gave you; do not turn from it to the right or to the left, that you may be successful wherever you go. Do not let this Book of the Law depart from your lips; meditate on it day and night, so that you may be careful to do everything written in it. Then you will be prosperous and successful. (Joshua 1:7–8)

After all God had done for them, all the wonders he had worked and miracles he had performed, he only asked one thing in return: to meditate on his law so they could live by it.

The act of meditating on the law would become one of the hallmarks of a righteous person, a person who loved and followed the Lord. Every time one of the patriarchs or prophets said, "The word of the Lord came to me," it was because as he was meditating on the words of God, and the Word showed up. Abraham was meditating on the revelation of God when the word of the Lord came to him and told him he'd have a son (Genesis 15:1–6). The word of the Lord came, not to a busy temple priest, but to a sleepy child, Samuel, whose only thought was to listen and obey — and that child grew up to become one of the greatest prophets of the Bible (1 Samuel 3:1–9). The word of the Lord gave Elijah the power to keep the rain from falling for three years as a judgment on Jezebel, Ahab, and their idolatrous people (1 Kings 17:1–2).

Meditation Throughout the Psalms

Of all the books of the Bible, perhaps none focuses as sharply on meditating on the Word of God as the book of Psalms. Each psalm is a meditation, a musical meditation on God's revelation of his love, power, judgment, and mercy. They are songs, many of them crafted by David, that repeat the saving works and words of God. The Psalms encourage us to meditate on God's Word continually, and through their pacing and repetition help us to do exactly that.

God also reveals the consequences of *failing* to meditate on his Word day and night. King David, who wrote more meditations focused on God's Word than any other Old Testament writer, failed to meditate on it in the hour of temptation, and so fell into terrible sin. He paid a high price for straying from it, for letting something else — his feelings for the beautiful Bathsheba — take the place of God's Word in his heart and mind.

David learned from his sins, though, and wrote down his meditations on God's revelation in his life. In his very first psalm, he cautions other believers not to make the same mistakes he did: "Blessed is the man who does not walk in the counsel of the wicked or stand in the way of sinners or sit in the seat of mockers. But his delight is in the law of the Lord, and on his law he meditates day and night" (Psalm 1:1–2).

Not only does meditation keep you from taking the path that sinners tread, it goes even further and actually brings delight to your heart. God isn't asking us to do this just to prove our obedience to him. That would be a good enough reason for *us*—he's God and we're not, so we should do what he says. But God wants more for us; not just to avoid sin, but to live in delight, joy, prosperity, and love.

David again expresses that kind of delight and satisfaction in Psalm 63. He begins with the image of a soul that is "satisfied with the richest of foods." Of course, at a rich feast you get everything you want and all your hunger is filled. This is what David is saying God does for his soul: when he meditates on God, he has everything he wants and his hunger is filled. He goes on to talk about meditation specifically:

> I will be fully satisfied as with the richest of foods; with singing lips my mouth will praise you. On my bed I remember you; I think of you through the watches of the night. Because you are my help, I sing in the shadow of your wings. (Psalm 63:5–7)

You can almost picture a dim, candlelit room, where a believer sits in quiet, intimate friendship with God as he meditates on him as you read this.

Several other psalms also offer beautiful imagery and wise instruction about meditating on God's Word. Psalm 77 shows us a believer meditating in a time of sorrow: "I remembered you, O God, and I groaned; I mused, and my spirit grew faint" (vs. 3), and "I remembered my songs in the night. My heart mused and my spirit inquired" (vs. 6). As a remedy to his sorrow, the psalmist decides that, "I will meditate on all your works, and consider all your mighty deeds" (vs. 12).

Psalm 119 is a great hymn affirming God's law and repeatedly praises meditation in the life of the believer. Verse 15 says, "I will meditate on your precepts and consider your ways," and a little further on, in verse 23, "Though rulers sit together and slander me, your servant will meditate on your decrees." Even when war and rebellion threaten him, this believer isn't letting anything get in the way of his meditation! He goes on to say later in the psalm, "I will meditate on your wonders" (vs. 27), "I will meditate on your precepts" (vs. 78), and "My eyes stay open through the watches of the night, that I may meditate on your promises" (vs. 148). This believer would rather meditate on God's promises than sleep through the night!

Meditation Throughout the New Testament

You're probably getting the idea by now that meditating on the Word of God is something God wants us to do. It's not just the Old Testament either that places this emphasis on meditation. Christians often ask themselves "What would Jesus do?" One answer to that is, "He would meditate on the Word of God!"

Jesus was a hard worker and a busy minister, but he still found quiet time where he could just open the words written on his heart and meditate on his Father's love. Matthew's gospel tells us that after feeding the five thousand, Jesus dismissed the crowds and "went up the mountain by himself to pray" (14:23). Meditation is a kind of prayer, one that Jesus did often.

In the first chapter of the Acts of the Apostles, after Jesus ascended into heaven, the twelve, Mary, and many other disciples gathered in the upper room to wait for the Holy Spirit to descend. For ten days they "all joined together constantly in prayer" (1:14), which would have meant both the traditional daily and weekly Jewish prayers and meditation on the Old Testament passages that foretold the life and work of Jesus.

Once the Holy Spirit came down on the disciples, they were given power to do many things: preach, teach, heal, speak in tongues, witness before kings and governors, keep the faith in jail and under persecutions, and to meditate rightly on the Word. In the power of the Holy Spirit, they were able to understand the Word rightly, not just with human understanding, but in the light of revelation.

A little further in the book of Acts (8:27–38), we see the difference between meditating in the power of the Spirit and trying to do it all on your own. A eunuch from Ethiopia had learned about what God spoke through Isaiah, and he was only experiencing confusion and frustration while meditating on it. But the Spirit wanted to open his heart and mind to the Word of God, so he sent Philip the deacon to show the eunuch how to meditate on the Word in the power of the Spirit. He showed him how the prophet was telling the good news of Jesus Christ, even centuries before Christ was born, and that's something that can only be known by meditation in the power of the Holy Spirit.

That's what the Word of God wants for us—to know the good news of Jesus Christ. Sometimes we know it through the touch of a brother or sister, sometimes through a teaching, sometimes through a miracle or the strength to go on one more day. And sometimes that good news is revealed to us in our meditation on the Word, because meditation opens a place for revelation. All revelation comes back to one piece of good news: Jesus is Lord. That's what all those Old Testament texts were leading to, all those psalms were singing about, and all those teachings by Jesus' disciples were proclaiming. When believers meditate on the Word, their lives proclaim it too: Jesus is Lord.

Chapter 6
Myths, Facts, and the Patterns of God

I love you—I am at rest with you—I have come home.
—Dorothy L. Sayers (1893–1957)

Prayer is the key to Heaven, but faith unlocks the door.
—Anonymous

Common Misunderstandings

We've seen that meditation is good for you, that it is a form of Christian prayer, and that the Bible not only allows it for Christians, but actually commands it. So why aren't more Christians doing it? Why are we in danger of losing this gift from God—the chance to be still and listen to him speak in our hearts?

I think part of it is that we have some wrong ideas about meditation. Maybe we grew up during the Transcendental Meditation movement, when everyone was saying that TM could solve all our problems. Maybe we associate meditation with non-Christian religions, especially if we've heard the stories of the Buddha receiving enlightenment while he sat meditating under a fig tree, or Muhammad meditating in a cave when the angel first started to recite the Qur'an to him. We might have images of skinny, bald monks sitting in the lotus position chanting "ohm," or long-haired flower children "meditating" on the universe with the help of a few illegal substances.

Here are some of the most common misunderstandings about meditation and the real answers to them.

>**Myth**: Meditation is just something you do to relax. I have better ways of relaxing.
>
>**Fact**: Meditation can be *relaxing*, but you don't do it *to* relax. You do it to enter into focused listening to God. Remember, it's not "doing nothing."
>
>**Myth**: You have to sit in the lotus position; and I just don't bend like that.
>
>**Fact**: You can sit in any position that's comfortable for you, but doesn't relax you so much you fall asleep! Meditation isn't about the position you sit in as much as it is about the position of your heart to receive from God.

Myth: When you meditate, you sit there and repeatedly chant "ohm."

Fact: Some people do that when they meditate, but Christians don't—and most others don't either. There are different types of meditation, and if you like to repeat a word or phrase, a "mantra," you'll pick a Christian one and focus on it instead of a sacred syllable from another religion.

Myth: Meditation is something people only do in other religions.

Fact: Nope. It's always been part of Christianity, we just don't hear about it much today. But there have always been Christians who meditate on the life of Jesus and the words of the Bible.

Myth: Meditation is a religious activity. Or, meditation can't be a religious activity.

Fact: Meditation can be religious, or it doesn't have to be. It's a question of how you focus it, and what you put into it.

Myth: Meditation is about emptying your mind.

Fact: Meditation is about choosing *what* to put into your mind. In Christian meditation, we choose to put in images and words from our faith; and we choose, for just a few minutes, to keep out the other things that are always trying to get in.

Myth: Meditation is only done by monks and nuns with nothing else to do all day.

Fact: Meditation is practiced successfully by many people as an important part of their busy everyday lives. You don't have to be a professional religious person to meditate.

Myth: Meditation puts you into a trance.

Fact: In a trance, you aren't aware of what's going on around you. But biblical meditation is about becoming more aware, not less. God wants you to listen to him, and you can't do that if you're zoned out.

Myth: Meditation is for intellectuals and brainy types. Regular people don't have much use for it.

Fact: Meditation is about getting closer to God. Anyone can do that, whatever your IQ. God would never ask you to do something he didn't make you smart enough to do. If he wants you to meditate, he gave you the ability to meditate.

Myth: Meditation is boring.

Fact: Meditation actually brings a deeper joy and attentiveness to life that transcends the small amount of time you actually spend doing it. It's true that at first it can be hard to sit still and listen. We're so used to being engaged and entertained at every moment that we often wrongly assume that a state of stillness or quiet is the same as boredom. It isn't, of course, but if we don't get some tangible rewards ASAP, we assume it isn't working or that it'll never work for us. But give it some time, so your patterns of thinking and experiencing can change. It won't take long — probably just a week or two, but soon the connection you get with yourself and God will make it one of the most powerful experiences in your life.

Myth: Meditation makes you passive.

Fact: "Just sitting there" seems to be in direct contrast to some of our cultural mantras, ideas that make it seem like "doing something" is the only way to do something. "Seize the day," "Go for the gusto," and "Act now" are all things we're told winners do. But who is more active than a soldier waiting for a commanding officer's orders, a mother listening for her child's voice, or a husband waiting for his wife to arrive home safely in bad weather? If your goal is a deeper relationship with Jesus, there's no better way to go for the gusto than to meditate.

If you think any of those myths about meditation, you're not alone. Most people, even Christians included, are surprised to hear that Christians do and should meditate. They think it's a New Age thing or something other religions do but not us. But from the time of Jesus on down, Christians have always meditated on God's Word, and as long as the Word of God is in our hands and the Word of God is in our lives, we always will.

Meditation, Recitation, and Manifestation

If you've spent some time with God, you've probably noticed that he tends to work in patterns. God is the same and he tends to work in the lives of humans in similar ways. One of those patterns will show up in the lives of anyone desiring to get closer to God through meditation. That pattern goes like this: meditation, recitation, and manifestation.

We've already talked about meditation, what it is and why it's important. But what's recitation? Recitation is saying the words God gives us until we've learned them by heart. Recitation is when the Word of God sinks so deeply into our minds and souls that it's there when we need it most—specific words for specific situations.

You probably already have some examples of recitation in your life. Most Christians know the Lord's Prayer, the prayer that Jesus gave us that starts with, "Our Father which art in heaven, Hallowed be thy name" (Matthew 6:9, KJV). Many people know Psalm 23 (KJV), which begins, "The Lord is my shepherd; I shall not want." Because those passages and prayers have been deeply meditated upon throughout history, they are there when needed. If you're ever afraid, if you ever struggle to turn over your circumstances to the Lord and put your trust in him, a few words from the Word of God brings the strength and comfort you desperately need.

> Even though I walk through the valley of the shadow of death, I will fear no evil, for you are with me; your rod and your staff, they comfort me. (Psalm 23:4)

> Who shall separate us from the love of Christ? Shall trouble or hardship or persecution or famine or nakedness or danger or sword? As it is written: "For your sake we face death all day long; we are considered as sheep to be slaughtered." No, in all these things we are more than conquerors through him who loved us. (Romans 8:35–37)

> Precious in the sight of the Lord is the death of his saints. (Psalm 116:15)

> Come to me, all you who are weary and burdened, and I will give you rest. (Matthew 11:28)

Of course, there are countless more promises than the above; the Word of God is full of verses, images, and passages that the Holy Spirit uses to speak straight to our heart. But how will you get them when you need them? When you sit at the bedside of a loved one being taken from you far too early, and you are aching for a word of comfort, how will you know the Lord has said, "Anyone who believes in me will come to me, and I will never turn him away"? And when your paycheck doesn't cover your basic living expenses, and you don't know how you're going to feed your kids this week, how will you remember the Lord's invitation to dinner, "Everyone who thirsts, come to the waters, and you that have no money, come, buy and eat"?

You have to let those words get inside you. Reading them is the first step, but you have to do more than *just* read. You have to read and repeat, read and repeat, read and repeat, until they are soaked into your mind, heart, and soul, ready for you to call up at any moment you need them—letting God's voice be your guide and comfort. That's what you're doing when you meditate. Imagine those words as a colorful piece of crocheted yarn; every time you meditate, you connect another thread of those words of power to the larger blanket of your life, until they are part of your existence, available to cover, protect, and warm you.

That's what recitation is—it's access to the promises of God when and where you need them. Reciting is simply saying with your lips the things you know in your heart. Recitation is the connecting point between thinking about something and doing it, just like the lips are the connecting point between the heart and the hands.

Recitation Steps

I want to show you how recitation works, whether we're talking about prayer or anything else. First you have a thought inside yourself. Maybe it's not exactly a thought, but a feeling, like a longing, frustration, anger, tenderness, or pride. Maybe it has grown there for years before you even knew it was there, or maybe it came to life in a flash of intuition. But it starts inside you, where only you and God know it exists. That's the meditation stage of things, whether we're talking about a relationship with the Lord or going back to school or helping a neighbor.

At some point that thought or feeling has to get from inside you to outside, because if it stays inside you it will always be a dream. Dreams have their place, but if they never come out, they'll never come true. So what happens next? At some point you *say*, "I've been thinking about taking a few classes," or "Mr. Jones looks awfully lonely since his wife died," or "I just wish my prayers were more meaningful."

Saying is the first step of recitation — *only* the first step though. Recitation is also taking God's words that you've meditated on in your heart and making a plan for fulfillment. It starts with just saying the need, inspiration, or dream, but it doesn't stop there. Just like God spoke a Word and the Word was Jesus, God didn't stop with Jesus just existing. God had an action plan. We don't know if God's action plan just came to him perfectly one day, with all the little details already in place, or if his plan grew in the back of his mind for thousands of years before the time was right to get to work on it. If you read the prophets of the old covenant, it kind of seems like God knew for a long time just what his action plan was.

You could look at it this way: God made some people, and he loved them, but they kept wandering away from him. And when God meditated on his people, he started to have a dream, or maybe just a deep feeling of longing, of wanting to be so close with his people that they could never be separated. They were already in his heart and he knew them by heart, but he wanted to be in their hearts too. God meditated.

But then God started reciting. God's recitation started by him telling people what his dream was: "They will be my people and I will be their God," and "I will break their hearts of stone and replace them with hearts of flesh," and "No longer will a man teach his neighbor, or a man his brother, saying, 'Know the Lord,' because they will all know me, from the least of them to the greatest" (Jeremiah 31:34). God's dream, his deepest desire was — and is — to bless his people. As he told us through his prophet Isaiah: "They will be called the Holy People, the Redeemed of the Lord; and you will be called Sought After, the City No Longer Deserted" (Isaiah 62:12).

The Word of God gives us thousands of examples of God reciting with his lips what he'd been meditating on in his heart. But God didn't just stop at telling the world what his dream was. He made an action plan, and he revealed pieces of the plan to us over time, through his prophets. Here's a bit of the plan that he told his prophet Isaiah:

> Therefore the Lord himself will give you a sign: The virgin will be with child and will give birth to a son, and will call him Immanuel. (Isaiah 7:14)

Here's another bit he told to Micah:

> But you, Bethlehem Ephrathah, though you are small among the clans of Judah, out of you will come for me one who will be ruler over Israel, whose origins are from of old, from ancient times. (Micah 5:2)

There are a lot more pieces of the plan God revealed over time. But you see that God didn't just lay around heaven with a dream in his heart. He spoke that dream out loud, then he made a plan to make it happen.

That's the second part of recitation: first you speak your dream out loud, then you make a plan to make it happen. So if you think you might want to go back to school, after you tell someone—or maybe just discuss it with the Lord—then you make a plan about how it's going to happen. It might look something like this:

- Call the community college and ask for a catalog.
- Think about how many classes you can afford and have time for.
- Think about which classes would be most interesting or beneficial.
- Call an advisor or enrollment counselor on campus.
- Get you family on board, reassign some responsibilities at home.
- Enroll in your course.

Now you've experienced recitation—you have a dream, you've spoken the dream, and you've made a plan for the dream. The second section of this book will be all about recitation; your choices, your action plan, how to take the dream of being with God and making an action plan so it happens.

Manifestation of the Dream

Sometimes we do all these steps without really thinking about it. If you've noticed that Mr. Jones seems lonely since his wife died, and you think you'd like to have him over for Sunday dinner, the next step is probably to look in your freezer to see if the roast you bought is big enough to feed an extra person. After that, you can call up Mr. Jones and ask if he's busy Sunday after church. If Mr. Jones is elderly, maybe you arrange for one of your kids to go get him and walk with him. Nobody had to tell you how to bring that thought to light or how to make a plan that fits your thought. You just know what to do. We do this every day—we take things from meditation, through recitation, and finally to manifestation.

Manifestation is what happens when the dream in your mind comes true. It's what happens when Mr. Jones is sitting at your table Sunday afternoon. It's what happens when you find yourself sitting in that classroom twice a week, learning about things that interest you. It's when the thoughts, feelings, and words that come up and come out during the first two parts of the cycle become actions and realities. It's when something that wasn't real becomes real. It's when something changes.

Any time something gets done, that's manifestation, and it doesn't happen without first meditation and recitation. This is even more true for meditation as a prayer practice. After a week or two of meditating, there will be a lot of manifestation going on. You'll be quieter in your heart and mind, you'll hear the Lord's voice more clearly, you'll start demonstrating the gifts of the Spirit in your life, and you'll be healthier. The third section of this book will be dedicated to manifestation, what happens when meditation takes root in your heart, mind, and body, and what is going to change in your life.

The Role of Faith in Meditation

There are two aspects of faith in regards to Christian meditation. These two aspects are "faith for" and "faith in." During your time of meditation, these two aspects of faith will work hand-in-hand. The "faith for" aspect derives from the Greek word *pistis* which means conviction, or persuasion with corresponding action. When you have "faith for" something you must demonstrate conviction and persuasion that whatever it is you are believing for will manifest. The "faith in" aspect derives from the Greek work *pistevo* which means believe, commit, to trust, or put in trust with. When you use "faith in" you are demonstrating your trust and commitment to God and his Word. David said in Psalm 20:7, "Some trust in chariots and some in horses, but we trust in the name of the Lord our God."

When you ask a believer what faith is, most would quote Hebrews 11:1 (NKJV): "Now faith is the substance of things hoped for, the evidence of things not seen." I contend that this scripture does not really tell us what faith is, but rather it teaches what faith does. Now then, a clearer understanding of this scripture is that faith becomes what you hope for until what you hope for actually comes.

For example, let's say you were remodeling your home and you needed some cherrywood blinds. You searched and searched and couldn't find the perfect blinds for your window. So you proceeded to search online and found the blinds that would be perfect for your windows. With great joy and anticipation you contact the company and order the blinds you need. We know they take your credit card as payment and email address and say to you, "Thank you. Your blinds will be shipped tomorrow. Please allow seven to ten days for delivery and your receipt will be emailed to you." Your receipt becomes proof you own the blinds. You may not have them in your house yet but based on your receipt you know they are on the way. Faith is your receipt that whatever you are believing for is on the way. I love the way Hebrews 11:1 is written in The Amplified Bible: "Now faith is the assurance (the confirmation, the title deed) of the things [we] hope for, being the proof of things [we] do not see and the conviction of their reality [faith perceiving as real fact what is not revealed to the senses]."

Are you afraid you don't have enough faith to meditate? Jesus says all you need to move mountains is faith the size of a mustard seed, and you already possess that. How do I know? Romans 12:3 exhorts us to think soberly, according as God has dealt to every man the measure of faith. As you meditate and recite the Word of God, your faith will be increased, strengthened, and matured. Romans 10:17 (KJV) says, "So then faith cometh by hearing, and hearing by the word of God." As you hear the Word preached/taught, it will cause your faith to grow. Your own recitation of the Word provides significant growth in your faith as well. If you want to expand in your faith, increase the amount of Word you hear and speak. Meditation helps you with both.

The biggest hindrance to meditation and prayer is not the *amount* of faith you have, but the mistaken belief that faith is what Mark Twain said it was: believing what you know ain't so. Many Christians say their prayers, read their Bibles, and meditate, but still harbor this secret suspicion that it doesn't do anything, that it doesn't make any difference. Some folks feel a bit blasphemous when they admit that to themselves, and yet they still suspect it.

It's not blasphemous to doubt. Doubt is natural. As a matter of fact, doubt is a precondition for faith, because, if faith is "relying on something *as if* it were so," then there exists the possibility that it isn't so after all — that you are, in fact, mistaken. You sit in a chair because you have faith that it will hold your weight, but you could be wrong. You could spill right out onto the floor. But you have to sit *first* in order to find out if you're right.

The biggest problem in meditating would be if you didn't meditate at all, because you aren't sure that it will do anything. Like sitting in the chair, you've got to try it before you render a verdict.

Try it. I contend that you'll find the time you spend with Jesus in meditation draws you closer to him, and that you'll see the fruits of your labor, the *manifestation*—not just in your spiritual life, but in your day-to-day life as well.

A Note to the Reader:
A Prophetic Message

As I was preparing these words, I received a word from the Lord. It is a word for all my readers, and so I am passing it on to you.

I sense by the Spirit of God that you are right on the verge of your manifestation and Satan is trying to get you to give up, to speak against what God has already spoken over your life, and trying to make you bless yourself because your waiting has been extensive.

But right now in the name of Jesus I take authority over the spirit of deception, anxiety, fear, doubt, mental torment, demonic oppression, seduction, mind control, illusions, and their manifestations, fruits, and demonic cohorts.

I command them to loose your mind, body, and spirit now in Jesus' name! I seal this deliverance by the Word, by the blood, and by the Spirit of God. In the name of Jesus! Amen!

I want you to now take a moment and praise God for your deliverance from these oppressive spirits and declare your freedom from them. Put the devil back under your feet where he belongs and continue to stand on the Word of God.

Hebrews 10:37–39 says, "For in just a very little while, 'He who is coming will come and will not delay. But my righteous one will live by faith. And if he shrinks back, I will not be pleased with him.' But we are not of those who shrink back and are destroyed, but of those who believe and are saved."

I declare that you will not draw back, but you will press forward into the plan and destiny God has for you. You will live by faith and receive the promises of God.

Section Two
Recitation

*For bear to judge, for we are sinners all
Close up his eyes, and draw the curtain close;
And let us all to meditation.*

—William Shakespeare, Henry v

Chapter 7
Forming the Habit and the Warfare Within

God cannot give us a happiness and peace apart from Himself, because it is not there. There is no such thing.
—C. S. Lewis (1898 – 1962)

Developing a Habit

As you start on this journey to obtain a more intimate and productive relationship with God through Bible-based meditation and prayer, I want to encourage you to be dedicated and committed to this new spiritual discipline. It is an essential ingredient to the success of every believer. As with anything else, the practice of meditation must be done consistently enough for it to become a habit. Theorists say that it takes twenty-one days to develop a habit. That's twenty-one days of doing anything—exercising, eating healthy, waking up early—will develop a habit in your life. They also suggest that when you want to start a habit, don't tell yourself you are doing it for life, tell yourself (with your conscious mind) that you are going to try it for only twenty-one days. Your brain will be more cooperative if you do.

For example, tell you conscious self that you are trying to start the habit of meditation for only twenty-one days. When you have completed this set time, your conscious mind has the choice of stopping it or carrying it on, or so it thinks. Your neural pathways have already re-formed and you will more than likely continue with your new habit. By this time you will have seen the benefits along the way and your subconscious will want to continue since it has been beneficial to you.

Talk to Your Spouse

After you talk to God about your new meditational time, it is very important for you to discuss your plans and schedule with your spouse. You should do this so there will be no misunderstanding in your relationship about what you are doing and why. For example, if you decide to meditate between four and five a.m., and every morning you get out of bed and go into another room without giving any explanation to your spouse, they are going to begin to wonder why you are leaving the bedroom for no apparent reason at that time of day. The Bible encourages us to abstain from the very appearance of evil and that no one should be able to speak evil of our good deeds (1 Thessalonians 5:22; 1 Peter 2:12).

You should talk to your spouse, sharing with them what you have learned about the power of Word-based meditation. Share with them your desired time to spend with God. Allow them to agree with you that the time you have chosen is a good time for the both of you. You don't ever want your spouse to feel like they're in competition with God. Your family is never in competition with God because God is a "family man" and everything he does is designed to enhance the family, not destroy it. Furthermore, by including your spouse in your decision, they may be inspired to meditate as well. Unity will always strengthen your relationship.

Active Resistance

Whenever you begin to make advances toward God you will always be engaged by spiritual warfare (demonic attack). Paul wrote to the Ephesians extensively on this subject, reminding them what they must do to stand against the attacks of the enemy:

> Finally, be strong in the Lord and in his mighty power. Put on the full armor of God, so that you can take your stand against the devil's schemes. For our struggle is not against flesh and blood, but against the rulers, against the authorities, against the powers of this dark world and against the spiritual forces of evil in the heavenly realms. Therefore put on the full armor of God, so that when the day of evil comes, you may be able to stand your ground, and after you have done everything, to stand. Stand firm then, with the belt of truth buckled around your waist, with the breastplate of righteousness in place, and with your feet fitted with the readiness that comes from the gospel of peace. In addition to all this, take up the shield of faith, with which you can extinguish all the flaming arrows of the evil one. Take the helmet of salvation and the sword of the Spirit, which is the word of God. (Ephesians 6:10–17)

I say this not to frighten you but to make sure you are aware of some of the things that may begin to occur as you take on the character and the mind of God through his Word. Satan can't stand the thought of you becoming the fullness of what God intended. Therefore he and his cohorts work overtime to discourage, distract, and derail you. Their primary goal is to hinder you from discovering the power that is in the Word of God through meditation. So each day before you begin to meditate I want you to pray this prayer of divine covering and grace:

> *Father, in the name of Jesus, you are the only wise God, full of grace and truth. To you be honor, glory, dominion, and power forever. You are my Savior, my Lord and my King; I worship you as I come into your presence. Father, I take refuge under the canopy of your love, grace, and protection. Shield me from all demonic attacks sent from Satan to distract, discourage, and derail me from my purpose in you.*
>
> *I command my mind, will, emotions, and body to come into divine alignment with the Spirit of God that I may receive all God has for me during this time of meditation. I declare and decree in Jesus' name that my mind is alert and my heart is open. My level of absorption is high and I am free from all demonic influences right now in the name of Jesus. Thank you Lord for your divine covering and protection in Jesus' name.*

The Warfare Within

The greatest warfare you will fight is the one within your own soul. Carnality versus spirituality are the two natures of man that are consistently at odds with one another. Paul reveals his own battle when he writes,

> So I find this law at work: Although I want to do good, evil is right there with me. For in my inner being I delight in God's law; but I see another law at work in me, waging war against the law of my mind and making me a prisoner of the law of sin at work within me. What a wretched man I am! Who will rescue me from this body that is subject to death? Thanks be to God, who delivers me through Jesus Christ our Lord!
>
> So then, I myself in my mind am a slave to God's law, but in my sinful nature a slave to the law of sin. (Romans 7:21–25)

The sin nature within us will always be an enemy of God. The only way to defeat the sin nature is to cut off its life source. The life source of carnality (sin nature) is any deed that is against the nature and commandments of God.

You must also guard the gates of your heart, which are your eyes and ears. They are the entrances to your spirit. If you want to defeat carnality you must begin to purify your environment by becoming extremely selective about what you watch (e.g. movies, websites, television shows, etc.) and what you listen to (e.g. music CDs, negative words from others, etc.). If you fail to make these changes, carnality will consume your life and undermine your destiny and purpose in God.

Paul reminds us that "the mind governed by the flesh is hostile to God; it does not submit to God's law, nor can it do so" (Romans 8:7). In other words, your carnal nature will never be able to comprehend or execute the things of God. Therefore you must strengthen your spirit by meditation, prayer, fasting, and by studying and hearing the Word of God; doing this consistently will defeat carnality in your life.

Effectual Prayer

I was raised in a church that had a strong emphasis on fervent prayer. As a product of that environment I learned how to pray fervently as a young child; but as I matured in my relationship with God I realized something was missing. I was spending a tremendous amount of time in prayer but I was lacking manifestation. I can't say there was no manifestation, but I knew there had to more than what I was experiencing. This realization was quite disconcerting, but I was determined to figure it out. I knew prayer worked so there must have been something that I was doing wrong. I asked God to reveal to me what I was missing and he immediately led to me to the latter part of James 5:16 (KJV): "The effectual fervent prayer of a righteous man availeth much." There it was; my answer jumped right out at me—"effectual." I was praying very fervently, but it was not effectual.

My next question to God was, "What makes a prayer effectual?" I searched for the definition of effectual and found that it means "producing or capable of producing an intended effect; adequate; valid or binding, as an agreement or document" (Dictionary.com). Suddenly I realized that the only thing that can make my prayers capable of producing, valid, and binding was the Word of God. That's what I was missing. Instead of praying the Word of God, which is the solution to my problems, I was rehearsing the problems over and over to God. Rehearsing the problems in your life will only exacerbate them. If you want the manifestation to your prayers, you must find the answer in the Bible and use it as your prayer to receive manifestation. There is nothing more fruitful and validating than the Word of God. Isaiah 40:8 (KJV) says, "The grass withereth, the flower fadeth: but the word of our God shall stand for ever." And Psalm 119:89 (KJV) declares, "For ever, O Lord, thy word is settled in heaven."

Consistent practice of Word-based meditation increases your knowledge and retention of Scripture so that, when you pray, your prayers will be based on the will and Word of God instead of your emotions. God does not respond to your emotions, he only responds to his Word. I had to realize that becoming emotional in prayer is totally fine. In fact, it's often therapeutic. But if you want to see the manifestation of your prayers you must make sure that your prayers are based on his Word. It is only then that they become effectual.

Chapter 8

A Checklist for Fruitful Meditation

There are many different ways to meditate, and as you seek to develop this discipline it will be through trial and error that you find what works for you. The practice of Word-based meditation can be as varied as the personalities of those who do it. Some prefer music during their meditation time while others prefer it to be completely silent, for example. As long as you develop the proper meditational techniques, you have the freedom to set your atmosphere any way you want; keeping in mind that your atmosphere must be conducive to the presence of God.

In this chapter we will go through a checklist to make sure you have everything you need to begin a life of effectual meditation. I will also share some of the details of my prayer and meditation sessions as well, giving you personal examples to encourage you in your journey.

Personal Example of Meditation

My time of meditation and prayer always begins with singing a worship song, or singing his name over and over again. Psalm 100:2–4 (KJV) says,

> Serve the Lord with gladness: come before his presence with singing. Know ye that the Lord he is God: it is he that hath made us, and not we ourselves; we are his people, and the sheep of his pasture. Enter into his gates with thanksgiving, and into his courts with praise: be thankful unto him, and bless his name.

Maybe you don't sing; and that's okay. During the times when I don't necessarily have a song on my heart I usually put on a CD of soft praise music. I listen to artists such as CeCe Winans, Clint Brown, Vicki Yohe, and Donnie McClurkin, just to name a few. The music must be quiet and nonintrusive for me, transitioning my mind to thoughts on the goodness of God, his love for me, and my need for him. The soft worship music helps me move from my regular life to this special time with God.

As the music plays quietly, filling the room with praise, I sit on the floor and get comfortable, close my eyes, and begin to breathe deeply and slowly. Some days it's easy to rest my head in the Father's arms, like a child on its mother's breast. I know without a doubt that's where I belong. Some days the unfinished business of yesterday and the anxieties of today crowd my mind, making it hard to create a quiet space for the Lord to speak. I often push back the distractions and return my concentration to my breathing or to the music.

Once I'm centered and focused — or as centered and focused as I'm going to get — I might do a few different things. I might just keep doing what I'm doing, breathing and listening. It's easier than you might think to spend twenty or thirty minutes being quiet and still with the Lord, especially when you and he have been having these meetings for a while. After I feel that my mind is connecting to the Spirit of God, I turn the music off because this is time for only he and I. Then I begin to either call his name repeatedly or say a praise repeatedly (e.g. hallelujah, thank you Jesus, or I love you Lord). From there he begins to speak and gives me instruction, encouragement, or leads me to a scripture in his Word.

Sometimes I pick up my Bible at this point. Maybe I feel a need for comfort, strength, courage, or discernment, so I might turn to some of those passages and edify myself with God's Word. Maybe God has planted a verse in my mind and I look it up. Once I get to it, I might understand what God is trying to say to me, or I might not. There are times I can't figure out why God put that verse in my heart, but later in the day something happens that causes me to understand why God whispered those words in my ear. I also often make my way, a few verses at a time, through some books that are important to me, like Psalms, Romans, or the 1 John. I might open up the Bible and read the next few verses — reading them slowly and repetitively in time with my breathing. And every now and then, I just open the Bible at random, hoping that God will surprise me. Sometimes I can't find anything meaningful on my random page, but sometimes I do.

Finally, when my meditation time is over, I close the Bible, stand and stretch, take one more deep breath, thanking God for always being with me, and walk out the door.

Your meditation time might look a lot like this, or it might be quite different. Your prayer won't be wrong just because it doesn't look like mine. I do want to explain, though, why I chose these patterns and why I think they could be very good choices for you. After all, it's not that the methods are right because I use them; I use these methods because they work for me.

Checklist for Fruitful Meditation

Every Day

Whether you meditate for three minutes or three hours, the most important thing is consistency. Remember the girl at her piano? Like her, you have to show up day after day—preferably at the same time—in order to start seeing meditation's results in your life. Your body and soul will start to anticipate the time, and they'll work on their own to get you into a ready state for your time with the Lord. Consistency is the key.

Morning

Meditation can take place any time of the day. But there's something special about the morning for me. The early morning is a quiet time; it's the quiet of the world as it gathers its energy, as it takes the deep breath that will energize it for the busy day that's coming. The dawn is a metaphor for the coming of the Lord into history and into our lives. Psalm 5:3 says: "In the morning, Lord, you hear my voice; in the morning I lay my requests before you and wait expectantly." And Psalm 30:5 declares that "weeping may stay for the night, but rejoicing comes in the morning."

Peter tells us in his second letter, "We also have the prophetic message as something completely reliable, and you will do well to pay attention to it, as to a light shining in a dark place, until the day dawns and the morning star rises in your hearts" (2 Peter 1:19).

Those few scriptures are just a small sampling about the importance of the morning hours. From the beginning of revelation, believers have compared the coming of the light after the darkness to the coming of God's light into the darkness of suffering and sin. And yes, there are certainly scripture verses that commend prayer and meditation in the evening and at night, because they are beneficial times as well. But there's something particularly meaningful about greeting the Lord as you greet the day.

Another reason morning is such a powerful time to pray has to do with the offering of our lives to the Lord. We're to offer God our best, not our leftovers. We're not supposed to squeeze meditation in wherever we can; our relationship with God comes first, and everything else gets worked in around it. As it says in Exodus 23:19, "Bring the best of the firstfruits of your soil to the house of the Lord your God." It makes sense that the firstfruits of the day are the first hours of the day, before all the fruit gets bruised by the cares and hassles of life.

It can be a challenge to dedicate time in the morning to meditation. Many of us don't consider ourselves morning people and we're afraid that we might not be awake enough to give the Lord our best. It's okay to have a cup of coffee or splash some cold water on your face first. It's also not the end of the world if you fall asleep—what could be more natural than a child of God falling asleep in his Father's presence? But, of course, you're not there to sleep, so you might find that dedicating some morning time means making a few changes.

I knew of a lady who was committed to meditating in the morning since it was her most energetic, focused, and clear-headed time of day. She had been in the habit of going to evening movies with her friends, but she found that the next morning, when she tried to meditate, the movie from the night before kept replaying itself in her mind. She tried for a while to just ignore the thoughts, but it soon became clear that it wasn't going to work. Instead, she told her friends that she could no longer go to evening movies, but she'd still go to afternoon movies. She had to make a few changes to her life in order to keep her commitment to meditation. Maybe you'll have to go to bed a little earlier, or take a power nap in the afternoon to make up for the sleep you lost getting up earlier in the morning. But the most important part is to make time to meditate with God and keep that time.

A Room Apart

I know that not everyone is able to find a whole room in their house to be used for nothing but prayer. Any space can be made sacred, even if only temporarily, when you use it for meditation—just recall Susanna Wesley sitting in her kitchen chair. But having a room apart, even a small one like mine, helps you to get in that sacred mental space. You don't have to work as hard to overcome the distractions of regular life in a dedicated space. When I go into my prayer room, I don't see my son's toys or the dishes my wife asked me to do last night. Only one thing happens there, so that's all I need to think about.

If you can find a space that you use for nothing but prayer, that would be ideal. It doesn't have to be an entire room. Maybe it's just a corner of a room. Maybe your meditation time is the only time you sit in that wingback chair in the dining room, or your grandmother's old rocker. Maybe you can just turn a living room chair around and face the corner or the window.

The most important thing is to make the space special during your meditation time, removing the distractions. You absolutely can meditate sitting on the living room couch; actually, you'll probably be really comfortable and relaxed there. But can you imagine just settling in, getting your breathing rhythm down, feeling yourself drawing nearer to God, and then — "Are those Junior's socks on the floor again? That boy! I've told him a thousand times to put his socks in the hamper, but he just — Oh, sorry, Lord, I forgot. But you know how that aggravates me..." And all your breathing, all your good intentions, and even your special time with Jesus is gone — because even if you do get back into your rhythm again, you know that half your brain will be grumbling about those socks.

A Comfortable Place to Sit

It's important that you are both comfortable and alert when you meditate. You should have a chair you like, but that isn't so comfortable you doze off. If you sit on your living room couch, sit up straight — don't lie down with your feet up on the armrest! If you need support for your back or arms, you should have it; nothing will take your mind off the Lord quicker than your own discomforts, so don't give your mind any excuse to wander off. Some people like to use a kneeling bench — a sort of half stool, half kneeler that lets you be on your knees, but still sitting comfortably on your backside.

Since breathing is such an important part of meditation, wherever you choose to sit should support your posture. If you're bent over, slouched, or uncomfortable, you won't be able to draw deep, clear breaths that fill your lungs and spread that good oxygen all through your body. Your chair needs to help you sit with a straight line between your chin and your belly button, because that's how deep your breathing needs to go. Since I have really plush carpet in my prayer room, I like to sit on the floor with my back against my daybed for support. Some may prefer to sit on a mat on the floor, on a cushion, in a beanbag, or on a stool. You might have to experiment a little to figure out what works best for you; but remember the two most important things in whatever you choose: be comfortable and stay alert.

Soft Worship Music

Music is a way that we mark a space as sacred. It can set the tone for our thinking and feeling, and even for our breathing. When certain music is played in a space, the meaning of that space can change. Think about Sunday mornings — you come into the church building, see your friends, and walk over to talk to them to talk. "How was your week? Are you feeling better? Did you get that job? You wouldn't believe who I ran into!" That's good fellowship time, but when the organist starts playing, what do you do then? You hook back up with your husband or wife, find your seat, and get your heart ready to worship the Lord. By the time the organ piece is over, the choir is in place, the pastor is standing up front with his Bible in his hand, and you are in your seat, your heart ready to worship God. At the beginning of the song you were fellowshipping, but by the end of it you're worshiping. One piece of music can move you from one spiritual place to another.

No matter what kind of music you like best, your meditation music should be soft and quiet. I love a good raise-the-roof, shout-to-God praise song, where we rock with the Spirit, put our hands in the air, and dance — that's awesome in worship. But if the Lord's going to speak in that still small voice of his, then the music shouldn't drown him out.

Another great thing about soft worship music is that the words and melody are written specifically to bring you into the presence of the Lord. That's what Christian musicians do, it's their gift from the Holy Spirit. Soft worship music creates a mood of awe and intimacy. It wraps us in comfort and safety. It gives us a way to calm our thoughts and worries, because the music is meant for calming. It's meant for leading us to rest in the presence of the Lord.

You don't have to use music at all, especially if it distracts you. If you do use it, however, make sure it is anointed music created by believers. Music has a spirit to it, and often the spirit of the person singing or playing influences the spirit of the music. So make your music selections carefully. It can bring the presence of God; but it can also hinder his presence.

Deep Breathing

Meditation is the one practice all religions have in common. For thousands of years people have understood the value of quiet, stillness, and most importantly, deep breathing. Breath is life for the body, and if our breathing isn't adequate, our life isn't adequate. Think of people who have emphysema or COPD — their lives are limited, aren't they? They have to walk slowly and carry oxygen tanks around, and they can't do all the things they used to or that they want to. Think of a mother checking on her baby in the middle of the night. She stands as still as a statue in the dark room until she hears the one thing she's listening for—her child's breathing. To breathe is to be alive, to breathe well is to be healthy, and that's true for both bodies and souls.

Here's a little revelation God gave about breathing. In Hebrew and Greek, the languages the Bible was first written in, there's only one word that means "spirit" or "Spirit," "breath" and "wind." In Hebrew that word is *ruach*, first seen in Genesis 1:1–2, when God was about to create everything with his word. Look how many ways that gets translated in English:

> In the beginning when God created the heavens and the earth, the earth was a formless void and darkness covered the face of the deep, while a wind from God swept over the face of the waters. (NRSV)

> In the beginning God created the heaven and the earth. And the earth was without form, and void; and darkness was upon the face of the deep. And the Spirit of God moved upon the face of the waters. (KJV)

> In the beginning God created the heaven and the earth. Now the earth was unformed and void, and darkness was upon the face of the deep; and the spirit of God hovered over the face of the waters. (Hebrew-English Bible)

Why would all those Bibles translate that one simple verse so differently? It's because there's just one word in Hebrew: *ruach*. But in English there are three words: spirit or Spirit, breath, and wind.

It's not just in the Hebrew language of the Old Testament that we see those ideas coming together in a single word. Do you remember after Jesus was raised from the dead and he came to visit his disciples in the upper room? That story was written in New Testament Greek; and Greek has one word for Spirit or spirit, breath, and wind as well. The word is *pneuma*, like pneumonia (a breathing infection) or pneumatic (powered by air). The story in John's gospel (20:21–22) says Jesus "breathed" on the disciples:

> Again Jesus said, "Peace be with you! As the Father has sent me, I am sending you." And with that he breathed on them and said, "Receive the Holy Spirit."

Since Jesus is God manifested as the Son, he breathes the breath of God onto the disciples, and the breath of God is the Holy Spirit. Breath and spirit are the same. So are spirit and wind, as we see in the story of Pentecost, when a great wind blew and the disciples were filled with the Holy Spirit:

> When the day of Pentecost came, they were all together in one place. Suddenly a sound like the blowing of a violent wind came from heaven and filled the whole house where they were sitting. They saw what seemed to be tongues of fire that separated and came to rest on each of them. All of them were filled with the Holy Spirit and began to speak in other tongues as the Spirit enabled them. (Acts 2:1–4)

So when Clint Brown sings "Breathe on me, breathe on me…Holy Ghost power breathe on me,"[3] it shows he knows that the breath of God and the breath of life are Holy Ghost power. Jesus will say the same thing in John's gospel: "The Spirit gives life; the flesh counts for nothing. The words I have spoken to you — they are full of the Spirit and life." (John 6:63).

That's not even the extent of the connection between breath, spirit, and wind. Have you ever noticed that the words *inspiration* and *respiration* look and sound a lot alike? One means to get an idea or a revelation — *in-spir-ation* — to have the Spirit in you; and the other means to breathe — *re-spir-ation* — to draw breath again and again. Those words come from the Latin *spiritus*, which mean Spirit or spirit, wind, or breath. In a similar way, your *con-spir-ators* are those who have the same spirit as you and your *per-spir-ation* is the breathing of your skin. They are all connected.

The next section of this book, "Manifestation," will talk about how important it is to get enough oxygen. Meditation is good for your body. But it's not just oxygen you're breathing in, you're literally breathing in the Holy Spirit. And the presence of the Holy Spirit is what makes this *Christian* meditation and not something else. Breathing in the Holy Spirit helps you focus your mind and heart on the Lord, making your efforts acceptable to him.

A Cross on the Wall

For Christians, the cross is one way to announce what a space is for. Not every room with a cross in it is a meditation room, but many Christian homes hang crosses on the walls as a wordless way of saying, "As for me and my house, we will serve the Lord." A cross on the wall does that in a meditation room too. It also gives us a place to look during our prayers. If you keep your eyes open during meditation, which is perfectly acceptable, it's better for them to focus

---

3. These words are taken from Clint Brown's song "Breathe on Me."

on an object that reminds you of Jesus and draws you closer to him. You can even meditate on the cross, as we'll see further on. For people who are more visually-oriented, meaning they learn and think better through images than through words, the cross can speak a powerful word straight to their hearts.

A Bible on the Table

A Christian should always have a Bible within easy reach. That's especially true during times of meditation. Not all Christian meditation has to use a Bible, but the Bible is going to be your main source of connection with God. After all, you want God to say something, right? You're listening for *his* voice. God speaks in many ways—through our conscience, the beauty of nature, the words of a wise friend or loving parent, sudden inspirations, and slow growing ideas—but none of those are more clear or direct than the Bible. And the more you know it, the deeper you dive into it, and the more you will hear from it.

Twenty Minutes

I said earlier that you can get started meditating with just three to five minutes set aside each day. And I still stick with that advice: you can. The most important thing to bring to meditation is a seeking heart, so if all you can offer at first is three to five minutes, God will honor that. But it won't be long before you find that three to five minutes isn't enough; you'll be longing for more.

What if you were interested in someone, but that person lived in a different city, and all your communication was done over the phone? At first your conversations might feel awkward and strange. "Hi, yeah, you might not remember me. We met when you were in town at your cousin's party, I was there with my friend—well, he's not really my friend but I work with him—I was the guy in the plaid pants and glasses—remember? You do? Well, I just thought you were pretty, and I thought I'd call to, you know, say hi or whatever. Okay, I better go. Bye." Awkward and kind of painful, right? But what if she said not only that she remembered you, but that she's been waiting around the phone hoping you'd call? Pretty soon, that rushed, fidgety, five-minute phone call won't be enough. You'll relax a little and start talking for ten minutes…then ten minutes twice a day. Then you'll call on your cell phone on the way to work, then after work you'll talk for half an hour. Then an hour; and it still won't be enough.

That's how it is when people are falling in love, and that's what the Lord is inviting you into through meditation. He's waiting around for you to call, and if you feel awkward and aren't sure what to do or how to do it, it's okay. He's just really happy you called. Next time you won't feel so strange, you'll know a little more of what you're doing, and you won't be so self-conscious. You'll want to linger a little longer next time.

Twenty minutes is really the amount of time it takes to calm the body and mind, and to settle into the rhythm of breathing that will guide your meditation time. It's the amount of time it takes to dive deeply into a verse, passage, or prayer. It's an ideal amount of time for getting all those benefits of meditation we'll talk about in the next section. You can certainly work up to meditating for longer than twenty minutes if you'd like; Susanna Wesley did it an hour a day. But it's hard enough to find twenty solid minutes for meditation, and if you do it every day, it should be a good amount of time for bearing fruit.

Tips on Meditating

Here are a few tips to keep in mind as you meditate:

- Remember why you're there. The goal of Christian meditation is to deepen your relationship with the Lord.

- Start small — say five minutes — and work up to longer periods of time.

- Make a consistent schedule and keep it. Consistency is the secret to success in meditation.

- Find a way to transition into your meditation time. This could be playing music, turning off electronics, counting your breaths, or drinking a cup of tea — anything that moves you from regular space to meditation space.

- Mark your meditation space as sacred, at least during the time you're using it for meditation. Lay a cross in front of you, open your Bible on your lap, or play soft worship music in the background.

- Get comfortable so that you're not thinking about your body or its discomfort. But don't get so comfortable that you fall asleep!

It is my hope that I've given you some helpful hints to fruitful meditation throughout this chapter to help get you started. Meditation is not to be daunting, but a simple process of loving God and listening to his voice. I want to now go on and show you the many various types of meditation — a little something for everyone.

Chapter 9

Types of Meditation: Needs, "Mantras," Objects, and Mindfulness

> God loves us as we are, not as we should be,
> because none of us is as we should be.
> —Brennan Manning

Different Types of Meditation

There are many different ways to meditate. Some are ancient, tried-and-true methods that have been valuable for centuries. Some are made up on the spot by people who approach God with a willing heart but few ideas of what they're actually going to do. None of these are wrong, not if they're entered into with a desire for God. Just think of the rich diversity of believers in the Bible and throughout the ages. C.S. Lewis says, "The worldlings are so monotonously alike compared with the almost fantastical variety of the saints." Since we've seen that God wants *everyone* to meditate on his Word, there must also be a wide variety of ways to meditate.

Even if you think you know the best ways for you to meditate, it's still a good idea to try a few different ones. For one thing, meditation isn't really like anything else you do in your life. If you're a structured, organized person, you might find that a structured way of meditating is very effective for you. However, you might also be surprised to find that your quiet time with Jesus is the one place where you are free to follow your inner spirit wherever it leads. Or maybe you will change and discover that although you began your meditation discipline with strict adherence to a defined method, you gradually find yourself feeling so secure during meditation that you can relinquish all control to God, and let him direct how your time together will proceed.

The opposite may be true also. If you're the kind of person who shows up with no plans in mind, waiting for God to show you what's on the agenda for the day, you might do very well with an unstructured, free form of meditation. But you might also find that without a point of focus—a verse, image, or method—you continue to skate the surface of meditation like a water bug on a pond. Perhaps God will use your natural spontaneity as a tool to further his relationship with you, or perhaps he thinks you're being presumptuous. After all, if you don't put in some work and expect God just to show up because you showed up, you might be putting God to a test he isn't willing to take. He may not be willing to show you any benefits until you've proven you're willing to put focus and submission into your meditation.

That's why it's always a good idea to experiment with your methods, your schedule, and your patterns. You may not know yourself and how you meditate as well as you think you do. Try different forms, and instead of deciding how you will proceed, succeed, or react, let the Holy Spirit show you those things. Instead of telling God how you are and how you're going to be, let him tell you and reveal things to you and about you that you've never realized before.

Differing Needs

Another important thing to remember when you're trying out new methods of meditation is that you won't always have the same needs from day to day. Perhaps you find a great deal of benefit in working your way through a Bible passage verse by verse, and that's what you do most days. That doesn't mean you have to do it every day, and in fact, you should have some other tools in your meditation toolbox. What if there comes a day when you're stricken by grief, as I was when I first began to meditate, and you simply want to weep on the Lord's shoulder? What if you are being oppressed by temptation and you need to wrestle with that demon in the presence of God? What if the Spirit is nagging at the back of your mind to look up some verse that you hadn't given any thought to in a decade? You need to have the ability to do those because God is in charge of your meditation and he'll guide you where you need to go.

On the other hand, just because you can change methods doesn't mean you need to skip around every day. Consistency is the key to successful meditation. You might get bored or restless, but faithfulness and commitment mean sticking with it even when it's not exciting or fun. If you don't, you'll never go as deep into the Word as he is calling you to go.

Think about it in terms of family life: if you're committed to feeding your kids healthy food, then you do what you have to do to put a healthy dinner on the table every night. Night after night you cook good food and your kids sit down at the table and eat with you. But then, one night, you have to work late, your kids have games or activities, and there just isn't enough time to be everywhere you need to be. On that night you can get fast food and eat it on the way to basketball practice. One or two nights of doing something different isn't going to undo the benefits of years' worth of healthy family dinners at the table. It's only when your discipline changes or weakens that your overall health and success begins to decline.

It's the same with meditation. Find a practice that works for you, that lets you go deeper every day, and build more spiritual health as time goes on. If you do that, missing one day or changing methods in response to a need isn't going to undo your firm foundation. Just make sure you aren't making the exceptions the rule. It's too easy to start eating fast food every night.

You can see then that it's a balance of consistency and flexibility, discipline and openness. Here are some of the most powerful and popular methods of actually doing meditation. You might decide to try two or three of these, or you might make something of your own by taking pieces of each of them, combining them into a form that works for you.

A Willing Heart — No Method

For those who know the Lord and trust him, there's something profound about coming into his presence and waiting on him. You still want to follow the tips above, such as breathing deeply and sitting comfortably, but this unstructured kind of prayer can be like two friends meeting with no plans in mind for their evening. If you end up seeing a movie, great, or if you end up going out to dinner, that is also fine, just as long as you can be together. The Lord may have something in mind for your time together, such as a verse he's been wanting to show you, but he might be content just to sit quietly with you.

The truth is that we tend to reach for words because they give us something to do; but neither you nor God has to bring words into it at all. In fact many Christian mystics of the past and present feel that this is the ideal state of meditation; that when you don't need words, images, Bible verses, or music — when there's nothing in your mind but a wordless experience of God — only then have you achieved true meditation.

I wouldn't go that far; I don't think there's anything wrong with having a method, verse, image, or whatever you need to help facilitate your time of meditation. After all, sometimes when you meet up with a friend, you do have a plan. You meet up in order to go to a concert or visit a relative or try a new restaurant. The friendship doesn't suffer just because you made plans for how you'd like to spend the evening. And people need something to see and touch and think about, and yes, even something to do. This is why God sent his Son Jesus to live among us — we were struggling with only having an idea of God rather than a direct experience.

Structure and plans can be great, but so can unplanned times spent in nothing but the joy of each other's company. Sometimes life gets so structured and so planned that a couple might say to each other, "Let's not do anything tonight. Let's just stay home and be together." That works in meditation too.

You might say to God, or God might say to you, "Let's not do a Bible verse tonight. Let's just sit here and be together for a little while."

The most important points of meditation, in structured as well as unstructured times, are having a willing heart and showing up when you said you would. If you do that, God will bless your efforts, whether you come with a plan or not.

Unstructured meditation, when you show up without a specific plan in mind, can be very hard for some personality types, but that might be a reason why you should try it. It's probably not going to be very productive for anyone with ADD or ADHD; it's just too easy for people with those disorders to lose focus and forget what they came for. On the other hand, it can be very liberating and comforting to know that no matter how you struggle in the real world, here is one place where you can be sure your efforts are accepted and blessed.

Others who might benefit from unstructured meditation, where you just show up, breathe, and let God decide on the day's agenda, include people with high-stress lives. Single parents, bosses with a lot of job pressure, or overextended volunteers all feel like their days have to be organized down to the minute — and they do or a lot of things will fall apart and a lot of people will be let down. But in twenty minutes with God you can let go and let somebody else be in charge. For twenty minutes you can say, "You make this decision." And you can be sure the decision is what's best for you that day. It's the one time when you can put all your stress and anxiety in God's hands. It was Peter who said, "Cast all your anxiety on him because he cares for you" (1 Peter 5:7).

Counting Breaths

A slightly more structured form of meditation is the simple method of counting breaths. Counting breaths can have several different functions in Christian meditation. It can be a way to practice getting your body in the rhythm of meditation, as we did in the first section of this book. It helps get your mind used to being quiet, to slowing down, to focusing on one thing while letting everything else go. It helps get your thoughts aligned with your breathing.

It's also a great way to transition between life or another form of meditation. When you go into your meditation space, your thoughts may be scattered and full of the day's anxiety, but then you start your breathing and count perhaps ten or twenty breaths. By the time you are done with that, you've prepared your body and mind to go further into your day's meditation.

We've already covered this, but here is how you meditate by counting breaths.

- Sit comfortably in your meditation space.
- Think about the Lord and your desire to know him.
- Ask him to show up and to be with you as you breathe.
- Breathe in, and count "one."
- Breathe out, and count "two."
- Imagine that when you breathe in, the Holy Spirit is that breath, rushing into your body.
- Breathe in, and count "three."
- Breathe out, and count "four."
- Imagine that when you breathe out, you expel sin, distraction, and worry.
- Breathe in, and count "five." And so on.

Again, this can be an excellent form of meditation for beginners, those who are easily distracted, those who have a million thoughts that won't leave them alone, and for those experienced meditators who want to get back to the basics. It starts to build the muscles of meditation, and any athlete can tell you that you always have to work on keeping those muscles strong. If you neglect them because you think you're too advanced, you'll end up on the bench.

Mantra: Repeating a Praise Word

To use a mantra is to repeat a sacred word or phrase. The word "mantra" is actually from the Hindu religion, but the idea of repeating a sacred word has been in the Judeo-Christian tradition — the biblical tradition — for more than two thousand years. It is an easy way to control thoughts and breathing, as well as letting some idea or quality of God be absorbed into our spirit.

A mantra is just a simple tool to help you with your concentration. In some religions, a mantra isn't even a whole word, just a syllable or sound that is returned to again and again. It's a means of corralling your unruly thoughts.

When using a mantra, it is important to coordinate your word with your breathing. It's like counting breaths, but instead of numbers, you'll repeat your sacred word.

- Breathe in…think "Jesus."
- Breathe out…think "Jesus."
- Breathe in…think "Jesus."
- Breathe out…think "Jesus."

And that is really all there is to it. You are going to get distracted, especially in your first attempts at meditation, but you'll even get distracted after you've been doing it for a long time too. That's when the mantra really comes in handy. Your meditation pattern might actually look something more like this:

- Breathe in…think "Jesus."
- Breathe out…think "Jesus."
- Breathe in…think "Did I mail that check for the utility bill?"
- Breathe out…think "No, I left it on the front seat of the car…darn it."
- Breathe in…think "I'd better mail that on the way to work…oh, heck, I'm supposed to be meditating."
- Breathe out…think "Jesus."
- Breathe in…think "Jesus."
- Breathe out…think "Jesus."

You can see how a mantra to return to is very valuable — you simply let the distractions go and return to your point of focus, your holy word, your mantra.

Mantra's are usually a single word. The name of Jesus is an excellent one to use — and, of course, there are many names used to describe Jesus in the Bible, none of them being more powerful than the name of Jesus. You could also use some of the original Hebrew and Greek names used to describe God. I will list them here with their meaning :

- Jehovah — God is Yahweh
- Elohim — My Creator
- El Elyon — Most High God (Sovereign over all)
- Adoni — My Lord, My Master
- El Roi — God who Sees
- El Shaddai — God Almighty
- Jehovah Ezer — The Lord my Helper

- Jehovah Jireh — The Lord my Provider
- Jehovah Rapha — The Lord my Healer
- Jehovah Roi — The Lord is my Shepherd
- Jehovah Sabaoth — The Lord of Hosts
- Jehovah Mekeddeshem — Lord who Sanctifies
- Jehovah Nissi — The Lord my Banner
- Jehovah Shalom — The Lord my Peace
- Jehovah Shammah — The Lord is Here

Mercy, love, glory, justice, peace, and faithfulness are some qualities of God that we know about, and meditating on them can benefit us in two ways. If we meditate on the word "mercy," just as a simple word that works its way down into our soul, when our meditation is over we will become aware of God's mercy in our lives. We will see God's merciful hand in places we'd never seen it before. It's sort of like when you buy a certain kind of car, suddenly you begin seeing that model of car everywhere. It's not that those other cars weren't there before; it's just that now you have a greater awareness of that car because you own one. Meditating on God's mercy, or any other quality of God for that matter, even just by saying the word over and over as a meditation mantra, will cause you to notice the mercy of God that has always been there.

The second benefit of meditating on the qualities of God or using them for a mantra is that they will become part of our thinking. Maybe words like "mercy" or "loving-kindness" or "power" didn't come easy to you before. Maybe you struggled with talking about your faith without sounding too religious. But when you weave those words into your breathing and thinking by using them in your meditation, they suddenly start to mean something. They become *your* words, words that God has revealed to you as though he were revealing them for the very first time. You won't feel awkward using those words anymore because they've become part of you through your times of meditation.

Meditating on an Object

Another form of meditation is meditating on an object. Some people are more visual than abstract. They can't stand in the hardware store with a paint sample card, imagining what the living room will look like in a different color. They have to actually go home, paint the living room, and move all the furniture back in, and only then do they know whether they like the color or not. There's nothing wrong with that type of personality.

Some think in more concrete terms than others; that's how God made them. It does become a problem in meditation, though, because most people think of meditation as more conceptual—you sit alone in a room and think on the Lord Jesus, or a passage of Scripture, and you derive some benefit from it. In my experience, about half the people I've met are more visual than abstract, so meditation holds no fascination for them. As far as they can tell, meditation really does seem like just "sitting and doing nothing." There's nothing to hold their attention, and so they try it once, maybe twice, their mind wanders, their eyelids droop, and they fall asleep.

For abstract thinkers, however, abstract meditation works just fine. But for concrete thinkers, something more concrete is needed. In that case I recommend trying meditation with an object: a cross, a picture of Jesus, even the Bible itself.

God has made us as physical creatures; let's not apologize for that. He gave us five senses, and it's principally through those senses that we live and move and have our being. We surround ourselves with physical artifacts in order to stimulate our thoughts and memory—at home, at work, and even at church. If we can't sit down with Jesus for twenty minutes without our mind wandering, then we can use a physical object to remind us of who we are and whose we are.

Now, meditating with an object gets us into a thorny situation. Some people see it as idolatry—worshiping a physical object instead of the living God. But obviously that's not what I'm advocating here—meditation is going to lead you away from sin, not into it. Your worship isn't directed toward the physical item in front of you; it's directed toward Jesus. Just like a picture in your wallet reminds you of a loved one, or a hat your grandpa wore before he died makes you think of better times, or the leaves pressed in a book remind you of an afternoon walk long ago, a physical item can be used to stimulate your thoughts and direct them Godward. Don't be concerned about committing idolatry. If your intention is to intensify your love for God and spend more time with him, then using an object to help you do that isn't going to offend him.

Meditating with a physical object helps us keep in mind what we're doing and who we're spending time with. Simply begin by choosing an object. It can be something specifically spiritual (again, like a picture of Jesus, a cross, or a molding of praying hands), but it doesn't have to be. Sometimes meditating on the goodness of God can be aided by choosing one of his good creations: clouds, for example, or a tree. After all, he made those things for our enjoyment.

A fruitful afternoon of meditation can take place just looking across a scenic panorama — "Where were you when I laid the earth's foundation? Tell me, if you understand. Who marked off its dimensions? Surely you know! Who stretched a measuring line across it? On what were its footings set, or who laid its cornerstone" (Job 38:4–6) — or a gorgeous sunset — "The heavens declare the glory of God; the skies proclaim the work of his hands" (Psalm 19:1).

Spend some time considering the object. Does it call to mind any scriptural references or the lines of a favorite hymn? Does it speak to you of some aspect of God's mercy and goodness? If you're meditating on a cross, perhaps you're put in mind of Christ's sacrifice on Calvary; if you're meditating outdoors, maybe the seven days of creation.

Follow your thoughts in a godly direction. For example, it occurs to me in meditating on a beautiful scenic view that "I am fearfully and wonderfully made," just as the vista is (Psalm 139:14), and the delight I receive from the view might be something like the delight God takes in me when my heart is pure and I'm full of the Holy Spirit.

Sometimes you will consider an object and nothing will happen; you sit for twenty dull minutes and that's all. Don't despair! God regards the thoughts of our heart. If our intention was to spend twenty minutes in God's presence, then we *did* spend twenty minutes in his presence, even if nothing outwardly productive came of it. We can't expect profound insights to arise every time we sit down to meditate. Just like spending time with your spouse or a friend, nothing may happen outwardly, but the bonds of affection are strengthened and the relationship is deepened.

Sometimes you will consider an object and your thoughts will tend in an ungodly direction — maybe toward money problems or family problems or work problems; or it might be toward the secret sins of your heart. Don't get up and walk off. It could be that God is inviting you to bring your burdens into his presence. Maybe he wants to take them from your shoulders; maybe he wants you to lay them at his feet.

Meditating with an object is a fruitful form of meditation. If you're more visual than abstract, consider the physical objects God has given you as a means to entering a deeper relationship with him.

Mindfulness

Mindfulness is a style of meditation that is concerned with paying attention, or being aware. In some ways it's a technique best practiced outside of your meditation space, but it can certainly begin in your dedicated meditation time.

Inward

Mindfulness has two separate focuses—inward and outward. To meditate for inner mindfulness is to ask for self-knowledge, for the gift of paying attention to your own thoughts, feelings, patterns, and reactions. Sometimes it will result in uncovering pain, but remember, God must shine his light on your pain in order to heal it. Other times you may enter your meditation with a question for the Lord, a desire to understand yourself so that you may submit everything within yourself to him. In that case, the best thing to do is just to ask, and then pay close attention to the revelations that bubble up.

Perhaps you say, "Lord, why do I get so anxious about money? Why is it so hard to trust you in this area?" Then you leave the question in God's hands as you continue with your breathing. Breathe in, breathe out, and think about the question. Recall how you feel when your paycheck comes and you realize it will barely cover your basic expenses. Keep breathing, slowly and carefully. Pay attention to your mind, your heart, your stomach, your shoulders—where the tension that comes with anxiety is often stored. That's your body's way of hanging on to anxiety—just let it go. Relax your shoulders and stomach muscles, roll your neck a little, and keep breathing deeply. If you pay attention to yourself—if you are mindful—God will show you what you need to know.

It won't be long before inner mindfulness is a normal part of our lives. We'll be aware that we're getting anxious before it becomes a problem, because our minds have been trained to pay attention through meditation. We'll realize what triggers our tempers or our sadness. In some cases we might become so aware of our bodies and minds that we'll come to understand that we are ill, in need of a counselor, or require help from someone else.

One believing sister experiences moments of meditative mindfulness in her work day. She says, "My job is pretty mindless and I tend to sit and dwell on things that bother me all day. Sometimes I get pretty worked up. This happened the other day, and my emotions were so riled up I could hardly stand to sit still; I knew I had to train my thoughts on something else.

"I began to focus on the texture of things against my fingers, what my breathing sounded like, the noise my coworkers made, the temperature of the air. I took in colors and inventoried how various parts of my body felt (hungry stomach, strained wrists, maybe my foot fell asleep). I made a point to think of nothing but what I was physically experiencing with my senses—all of them.

"All in all, it's really hard to maintain for longer than a minute or so, but I think with practice it could become really effective in calming my thought life, and even train me to be more diligent in my prayers."

Outward

Outward mindfulness is very similar to inward mindfulness, except it trains us to pay attention to the people and things around us. We might start this sort of meditation simply by asking God to show us who we can help today—and we might be surprised by his answer.

A friend of mine was convicted to be more faithful in seeking outward mindfulness by some dealings she'd had with a colleague. The other woman was difficult, short-tempered, and impatient, and my friend was nurturing some bad feelings about her. One day the woman disappeared from work, and my friend didn't ask why—she was just grateful for the break from the colleague's bad attitude! A few months later the woman returned to work, and was as pleasant and helpful as she could be. My friend learned that before her absence from work, the woman had been in agonizing pain from a back injury, and it was all she could do to get through the day, but during her absence had undergone a much-needed surgery that helped relieve the pain.

"I should have paid better attention," my friend said. "Maybe God put her here so I could help her, and all I ever did was complain about her. I had to repent of that both to my colleague and to the Lord, and ask him to help me be more mindful of the people around me."

That kind of mindfulness can be cultivated in meditation. It comes from a mind open to receiving what God sends our way as well as a heart open to God's leading. It comes from our eyes being open—both the eyes of the face and the eyes of the heart. We can learn those godly skills through meditation, learning to be mindful of those God has put into our lives. Let us now turn our minds to a different type of meditation: biblical meditation.

Chapter 10

Types of Meditation: Biblical Meditation

Lectio Divina (Divine Reading)

Don't be fooled by the title—it's Latin, but that doesn't mean it's hard. *Lectio divina* literally means "holy" or "divine reading." It's a method of Christian meditation which not only brings us closer to God, but also increases our knowledge of the Holy Bible. It is simply reading a Bible passage meditatively, contemplatively, reflecting on its meaning and praying for it to become a part of who we are.

The steps are simple and straight-forward. Anyone can follow them. They are:

- Reading
- Meditation
- Prayer
- Contemplation

These steps aren't meant to be rushed through however. They are meant to be taken slowly, like a peaceful and meditative meal, except the taste we're savoring is the sweetness of God's Word. In fact you can think of the whole process in terms of eating:

- We take a bite (reading);
- We chew on it (meditation);
- We savor it (prayer); and
- We digest it (contemplation).

We'll break down these steps further on, but let's first talk about where, when, and for how long this method can be practiced.

Getting Ready

Some people practice *lectio divina* for one continuous hour a day. That's praiseworthy if you can do it, but it will be just as rewarding if you can do it for a shorter amount of time only a few days a week. Make sure to choose the time of day when you're most alert, and a day of the week when you won't have too many concerns pressing in on you from outside.

Choose the passage of Scripture you're going to read before you sit down to meditate on it. Several minutes can be lost just flipping through the pages, trying to find something that strikes you as "just right." Is there a right way to choose the scripture you're going to read? Not really; any method will work. You might have a list of favorite passages and work your way through them. Or, if you prefer, you can turn to a favorite book and open it at random. The whole Bible is God's Word and every part of it is profitable. Obviously, some parts are more accessible than others. I would recommend starting with one of the gospels or maybe Paul's letter to the Romans. Moving through a whole book, passage by passage, is an excellent way to "meditate through" a book of the Bible.[4]

I keep using the word "passage," but what does that practically mean?

Remember when your mom used to tell you to slow down at dinner and chew your food? She had two motives: she wanted you to taste what she cooked, and she didn't want you to choke. In *lectio divina* it's best to take small bites of Scripture. In his Holy Word, God has set before us a veritable feast, and he wants us to appreciate it. A passage that's too big will choke us — there's too much to consider, too many messages all at once. We'll be overwhelmed. Depending on the version of the Bible you use for meditation, passages might be set apart in paragraphs, with bold-faced subtitles. If you're using a Bible that runs everything together, you might just read until you come to the "turning point" in the reading: that place in the story or the letter where you sense a new point is being made.

Before you start a session of *lectio divina*, make sure you're sitting in a comfortable spot, free of distractions. Take a few cleansing breaths and pray for the guidance of the Holy Spirit. Then open the Bible and begin.

Read the Passage Slowly and Attentively

You may have to read the passage several times to get the full flavor of it. If it helps to keep your mind from wandering, you might write the words down

---

[4]. I have also put a list of good passages for meditation in Appendix C at the end of this book.

in a journal, so you can go back and consider each one when you're ready. There is no wrong way to read the scriptures, as long as it's done slowly and contemplatively.

Ruminate on what You've Read

When you find yourself lingering over an image, a phrase, or a word, then stop and ask the Holy Spirit to enlighten your heart. Do not be disappointed if you do not gain a special insight or revelation; revelation may come, but it also may not. The point is not to gain insight; the point is to taste the feast God has prepared for you. Take several deep breaths and roll the word or image around in your mind.

Speak with God

Think of prayer as a loving conversation with God. Thank him for the feast, for the care with which it's been prepared, for the opportunity to sit with him. Thank him for this morsel in particular. Share with him the thoughts that arise, the hunger that lies deep within. Allow him to touch you, to change you at the core of your being.

Gaze upon Him

Set your eyes upon Jesus in simple, wordless prayer. Feel the fullness of his Word. Rest contentedly, like you used to do after Sunday dinner. When you're ready, emerge from your prayer time by getting up and moving around. Then feel the joy of a satisfied heart. Let the Word penetrate you and energize you for the work you have to do.

Lectio divina is the oldest form of Christian meditation, and it's fruitful whatever your educational background. Don't let your unfamiliarity with Scripture keep you from engaging the Bible in this wonderful, satisfying way.

Meditating on a Bible Passage

Lectio divina is one way of meditating on a Bible passage, but there are other techniques that you might want to try as well. As I said above, when you choose a passage, it should be fairly self-contained, and preferably short. Every word, phrase, and story in the Bible has so much meaning to it that you could meditate on the same passage for a year and never exhaust its meaning. So don't try to do too much all at once.

It's especially important and effective to meditate on a passage you think you know really well. We often block our spiritual ears by our assumption that we know what a story means and that we have nothing more to learn from it. How many times have we heard Psalm 23 or the story of the prodigal son? It's likely we've heard them so many times that we don't bother or aren't able to hear God speak a fresh word through them. And yet, when God changes our hearts, he changes the impact of the stories we know by heart.

Choose a passage, part of a passage, or a story to begin. If you plan to meditate on a long passage, such as the parable of the prodigal son, break it up into pieces of action. You might start with meditation on the first part, how the younger son was irresponsible and disrespectful toward his father. It won't be long before meditation on that young man's actions provides a mirror of your own, and God will show you how you have been irresponsible and disrespectful toward your Father. The next day you might meditate on the second part, how the father shows mercy to the disrespectful son, and ask your Father to show you mercy in a similar way. Finally, meditate on the conclusion of the story and how the father's faithful child doesn't always appreciate mercy shown to others. Have you resented the mercy and grace poured onto others who don't seem to deserve it? We all feel that way sometimes, but our Father's love is big enough for all of us. That's just one example of how you might split up a long story or passage into manageable parts.

Before you begin, center yourself and get yourself into a meditation-ready state by breathing deeply or counting breaths. Counting ten breaths should help you to be calm and focused. One way to meditate on a passage is to read it aloud, in time with your breathing. Keep your breathing measured and steady, keep your words in time with it. When you get to the end of the passage, begin again, keeping your breathing steady. While your attention is directed toward your reading and breathing, the hidden messages of the passage will be working their way deep inside you. You might have a revelation much later in the day, when the meaning pops back up, clear and true.

Another way to meditate on a passage is to read the story a few times through, either aloud or quietly, and then simply set the Bible aside and begin breathing. You don't have to ask, expect, or require anything. Just let the words exist as you concentrate on your breathing. Sometimes the words will fade away, but sometimes they'll plant a seed that will grow as you meditate. Let the Word of God operate under its own power; your job in this technique is simply to breathe—to give the Word the spiritual nourishment it needs to take root and grow.

Meditating on a Bible Verse

Meditating on a Bible verse is similar to meditating on a mantra, a repeated Christian word or phrase. You choose verses of similar length, matching your breathing, and you repeat them in time with your breathing. But meditating on a Bible verse is slightly different from meditating with a mantra, even if the mantra is a phrase. The point of a mantra is to keep your mind from wandering, to come back to a holy place, keeping your breath going, and being ready for anything the Lord sends. However, the point of meditating on a Bible verse is not only rhythm and focus, it's also to let that verse sink deep inside you, until you know its truth like you know your own name.

Sometimes you will choose your verse based on what you are feeling that day, or what God has revealed you need to do in meditation. If you know your faith needs to be strengthened, you may pray the verse from Mark's gospel, "I do believe; help me overcome my unbelief" (Mark 9:24). If you've been struggling with keeping your temper around your spouse or kids, you might pray, "Love is patient, love is kind" (1 Corinthians 13:4) If you've been having a hard time detecting God's presence in the movements of your life, you might meditate on, "And we know that in all things God works for the good of those who love him, who have been called according to his purpose" (Romans 8:28). You're likely to finish your mediation with a deeper trust in God, even if you can't clearly see what he's doing right now.

Sometimes, however, God will choose the verse for you. He might communicate his choice in a couple of ways. You might be settling down to another form of meditation, counting breaths or using a mantra, and as you begin to focus, you may receive specific thoughts or verse numbers. You'll often experience these as intrusive thoughts that won't go away.

You might be sitting there, trying to meditate, and the activity going on in your head might end up something like this: "In (one)…out (two)…in (three)…out (four)…in…Psalm 91 (five)…out…Psalm 91…(six)…" Clearly there's something valuable for you in Psalm 91 and it would be worth your time to look it up, do some *lectio divina*, or simply meditate on the passage as described below.

God may even choose to give you a feeling or a longing for something that will direct that day's meditation time. Sometimes these longings are feelings buried deep inside, and sometimes they're feelings God plants in us to draw us to himself. So if you're lonely and wishing there was more love in your life, God might send you to the famous hymn of love in 1 Corinthians 13 to remind you what real love looks like. Or he might nudge you toward the declaration from 1 John 4:8 that "God is love." Further meditation might reveal John's preceding verse (4:7), "Dear friends, let us love one another, for love comes from God. Everyone who loves has been born of God and knows God." Perhaps you might learn that God wants you to work on loving the people around you rather than wishing for a romantic partner. If you're "loving one another," you're becoming more loving, and God may lead the right person to you at the right time.

Another way God might reveal a verse to you is through the random, close-your-eyes-and-open-your-Bible method. To tell you the truth, God doesn't use this method as often as people wish he would, because people tend to use it like magic, like a divining stick or an oracle. God's Word isn't a magic eight ball that you can direct questions to and get one-size-fits-all answers. Sometimes the answers are revealed deep in Scripture, or in that place where the Word of God lives in our hearts, and aren't very easy to find. One reason we meditate is to go down to the deep places where God speaks.

There are many times God intends to lead us to a verse we never could have found on our own. For example, I can think of a hundred different reasons why any one of us might need to hear the words, "Commit to the Lord whatever you do, and he will establish your plans" probably when we haven't committed like we should! But how many of us know that verse exists? How many of us know exactly where to find it? Even people who study the Bible day in and day out don't always know how to find what they need—or don't know what they need as well as God does! That verse is from Proverbs 16:3, pretty close to the middle of the Bible—a place you naturally open up to when you're using the random method.

Visualization: Placing Yourself in the Scene

Visualization is another form of biblical meditation that requires you to go deeper into the Word than ever before. Just like with *lectio divina*, you read a self-contained passage to begin: parables are excellent to start with, as are stories from the life of Jesus or Paul, or taken from the Acts of the Apostles. Genesis and Exodus have some great stories as well, as the prophets are always telling of the things God called them to do and say and the resulting actions of their obedience. There are even some prophesied stories in Revelation, stories of things that will happen, even if they haven't happened yet.

In order to visualize yourself in the scene, just like you would begin any type of meditation, read the passage slowly, timed with your breathing. Don't rush this part; just get to know the story, even if it already seems familiar to you. Read it through three times, slowly (there's no hurry here), breathing in and out, asking nothing more of it than the privilege of reading it. You might be tempted to skim over parts you think you know well, but if you keep your breathing steady and continue to return your focus to the words, you'll be able to resist that temptation.

Now mark your place and set the Bible aside. Focus on your breathing again. After a few moments of breathing, start thinking about the story you just read. Imagine it as a movie—how would it look on film? Where is everyone standing? What is the main character of the story doing? Is Jesus being yelled at by scribes or Pharisees? Where are they located—right up in his face, or keeping a distance? Is the lighting bright, perhaps to indicate the middle of a hot day in the Holy Land, or is it dim, such as at an indoor dinner or a garden by night? Are there close-ups? What is the expression on Jesus' face—is he frustrated, sad, angry, or infinitely patient? Spend several moments seeing the story happen without the screen of the words.

To bring this home, insert yourself in the story. Move beyond seeing it like a movie—actually be in it. Perhaps you could cast yourself as a minor character—a Roman centurion standing nearby watching for trouble, a faithful Jew who doesn't want to argue with the Pharisees, one of the apostles whose name doesn't get mentioned that often—James the Lesser or Nathaniel perhaps. I've always wondered if Stephen and Matthias were in the background somewhere, since they became such important followers after Pentecost; maybe you can imagine yourself as one of them.

Think about what the experience would be like. How do things feel? Is the sun hot on your face? Are your feet sore and dusty from traveling? Are you full and content from food and wine? What are the people around you doing? Are the scribes whispering among themselves to agree on the best arguments, or do they just shoot out Bible verses against Jesus, one after the other? What's the feeling in the air? Is it tense, because people respect the Pharisees and scribes, but they also like Jesus? Is it a mood of friendly banter, where everyone understands they're on the same side and debate is an enjoyable way to pass the time? Is it a mood of awe and humility, because most people sense that there's something extraordinary about Jesus?

What do you see now? Look at the people around you. Jesus' skin is probably darker than you've seen in paintings, and his legs are caked in dust up to his calves. The apostles look weary; they've been traveling far, energized only by their love for Jesus. Some anonymous people in the crowd look at Jesus with desperate hope—can he heal their illness or save their child? Are the Romans suspicious of Jesus, or are they cynical about the whole Jewish religion? Are there trees growing close by, buildings towering over, or are you out in the open, on a well-traveled road or the side of a mountain, trying to hear what's going on? Examine the details of the scene, and if the Bible story doesn't tell you what they are, imagine them. Visualize them, paint them with the brush of your creativity.

Let the story play out at this point, keeping in mind all of the details you just imagined. Imagine Jesus saying what he says, and the others reacting to him, in the way you've envisioned it up to now. Watch it all happen from your position in the story. And now pay attention: How do *you* react? How do you feel? When Jesus says, "Take off the grave clothes and let him go," does his voice ring in your heart as though you have been unbound and liberated? When Jesus pronounces to his followers, "You of little faith," does your heart ache because you know he means you? Participate in the story from your chosen point of view.

Learning and receiving from this kind of meditation will bring much transformation to your heart. It's a way to delve deeply into the Scriptures and the reality of the events we read about. They didn't happen in stained glass or in King James English—they were real people with real experiences. Our understanding of the Bible has to be grounded in the knowledge that the events happened to real humans, humans with dirty feet and growling stomachs and skin burning under the sun as well as insecurities, excitements, fears, and hopes.

It's also a way to open all your senses to communication from God through the prophets, saints, evangelists, and Jesus himself. Prayer isn't just about words meeting words. Prayer is something you do with *all* of you, smelly feet and squinty eyes and callused fingers and sensitive ears and a thirsty tongue. Put a body on that story, put some skin on that prayer. Jesus meets you in the reality of human life, not in some abstract place where only words exist.

Visualization is also a way for you to look Jesus in the eye, to touch his garment, to be in his presence. It's almost like time-travel, only it's not entirely clear whether you're traveling or Jesus is. Maybe you both travel and meet somewhere in eternity, where the life of the spirit is lived.

There are times when you're meditate on a Bible passage by visualizing yourself in the middle of it, and Jesus acts out the story differently. You don't have a right to change it, of course; your imagination needs to stick to the boundaries the Bible gives you. But he can change it if he has something else to communicate to you. A Christian brother of mine was praying this way once, meditating on a story where Jesus was teaching the crowd, imagining himself as a peasant who had come to listen to this new teacher. He wasn't changing anything as he felt the hot sun on his face, the rumbling of hunger in his stomach, and the blisters under his sandal straps. But suddenly Jesus stepped toward him, locked his eyes on him out of everyone else in the crowd, and a voice said, "What do you want?"

And the answer came immediately, "You!"

My friend never knew who said which part — or maybe he and Jesus stood in the crowd and made that declaration of loyalty to each other, both parts coming from both people. That wasn't how the story originally went, but that's what Jesus decided to do with it on that day, in the context of my friend's time of meditation. If you give Jesus the space to truly live in your heart, mind, soul, and imagination, there's no telling what he'll do once he's in there.

Visualization: Imagining God's Future Acts

We've talked about how important meditation is and how the fundamental purpose of meditation is simply to live in God's presence. But meditation can have another purpose too. In meditation you can open yourself up to receive answers to important questions. For example, when you ask someone who regularly meditates what he plans to choose in a given situation, he might say, "I'll meditate on that," in the same way the rest of us would simply say, "I'll pray about that."

We can meditate for discernment, strength, understanding, or for a need because we can pray about those things. Meditation, remember, is simply a form of prayer. In this kind of prayer you visualize how God will act and what your life will be like when he does. You picture God's decisive work as though it had already happened.

When you do this, you exercise faith. Hebrews says, "Now faith is confidence in what we hope for and assurance about what we do not see" (Hebrews 11:1). This kind of faith can be exercised through meditation. The things we ask for may be real on a level deeper than and higher than our senses can perceive. That's a level of reality only accessible by meditation. Through it we can see what it will be like when God is ready to make his promises real in a way that everyone can see. We can see what it will be like when our child is healed, we start a new job, our marriage is more loving, or a risky new ministry succeeds.

There are two great benefits to this kind of visualizing meditation. One is that it takes faith to assume that the reality we only have access to in our meditation is actually *the* reality of life. It isn't always a done deal to believe that just because we can picture God acting, that means that God will act or is acting. Visualizing meditation is a way to build up our own faith—a spiritual workout we all need from time to time. Our Lord only needs faith the size of a mustard seed to work with, but many of us fall short even of that. We have to do everything we can, including meditation on what God will do, in order to build up our tiny faith.

The other great benefit to visualizing God's future acts as though they were completed now is that when God does choose to make his acts real in the world of the senses, we'll recognize the hand of God when we see it. We've imagined it, watched it with the eyes of our spirit in meditation, and so when it does happen we'll know exactly what is taking place. We can declare to our friends, "Get ready, God's about to start the healing!" If you've ever known someone gifted with seeing the hand of God in everyday life, it's probably because they meditate on the future acts of God.

At times the thing we want so powerfully from God is not his will for us. People get scared and they lose the ability to submit to God's will, so they ask for things he's just not going to grant—not the way they want it, and not on the timeline they've set for him. That can also be dealt with in meditation. Ask God to reveal the image for you to meditate on. If you want healing for your child, instead of visualizing a picture of your wishes, ask God to show you a picture of your child made well. Once God reveals that image, then you can meditate on it. That way you know you're visualizing his picture, not your own.

Visualization is a popular meditation technique for those who are not religious as well. It's useful for people trying to clarify their goals in life, relationship issues, or anyone seeking physical or emotional healing. In Christian meditation we can do all of these things, bringing them to the Lord for his light to shine on them.

Here are some steps to effective visualization, borrowed in part from a non-Christian meditation teaching called Visualization Techniques, and modified for Christian prayer.

- Write down your goals or hopes — the outcome you are hoping for. If you'd rather not write, think of a few of the most important things, the ones you want most to see accomplished in your life.
- Find a quiet place, breathe deeply, and open your spirit to God's Spirit.
- Choose the most important outcome on your list.
- Once you are in a meditative state of focus and openness, ask God to show you how it will be when your desire is accomplished. Let your imagination wander freely because it is a gift from God and is often used to reveal his will.
- Ask God for the faith to accept as reality the prayer you are visualizing.

Visualization is ultimately an act of faith and requires you to believe with some part of your heart that God can and is willing to bring you the blessings you ask. It might require a lot of hard work from you as well, but being able to imagine it and see the result is a strong motivation. Visualization is an important way to meditate on God's Word and his will.

Now that we've discussed some breathing techniques, the importance of a willing heart, repeating a "holy word," and discussed various ways to meditate biblically, let us now turn our attention to some more ways we can meditate — creating an atmosphere of meditation.

Chapter 11
Types of Meditation: Music, Self-Examination, and Wrestling with Demons

> Not self-regarding, but God-regarding.
> It is not self-loathing, but God-loving.
> —Fulton Sheen

> The hermits went into the desert
> to take the war to the enemy.
> —Garrett Keizer

Meditating with Music

Some people meditate with music better than with a text or an object. That's not a problem: God makes all sorts and conditions of men. If music helps you turn your heart more fully toward God then, by all means, meditate with music. But be aware that not all music is going to enhance meditation: some will distract you and some will lull you to sleep. You need to be careful which type of music you choose for fruitful meditation.

Hymns

Hymns are the most obvious choice when it comes to meditating with music. A hymn is a meditation on some aspect of God's love, so it seems ready-made for using in our own times of prayer.

William Cowper, the great eighteenth-century hymnist, once wrote, "Sometimes a light surprises the Christian while he sings; it is the Lord who rises with healing in his wings." Singing a hymn slowly and meditatively so that you can concentrate on the words—or singing it at your own pace and losing yourself in wonder, love, and praise—can be wonderfully refreshing to the soul.

You're able to do this by taking only one line from a hymn, or one image, holding it in your heart, repeating it over and over again, singing it to God unceasingly. Consider the full meaning behind such well-known refrains as, "Crown Him with Many Crowns" and "It Is Well with My Soul." An entire morning's meditation could be taken up just meditating on the words of "In the Garden," which are as follows:

> I come to the garden alone
> While the dew is still on the roses,
> And the voice I hear falling on my ear
> The Son of God discloses.

And He walks with me, and He talks with me,
And He tells me I am His own;
And the joy we share as we tarry there,
None other has ever known.

Or you could meditate on the words of this popular hymn in the traditional African American Church, entitled "I Need Thee" (as recorded by Bishop Paul S. Morton):

Verse 1:

I need You like the ocean
needs the water or it will run dry,
I need You like the many stars above
needs the setting of the sky.
I need You like tomorrow
needs the hours of today to pass by;
Lord, I need You more than ever,
so hear my humble cry.

Chorus:

I need Thee, oh I need Thee,
every hour I need Thee.
Bless me now my Savior,
I come to Thee.

Verse 2:

I need Thee in the morning
when from evening's rest I wake,
I need You to direct my path in every step I take.
I need You, Lord to keep me,
I need Your mercy and Your grace,
yes, I need You more than ever,
You promised never to forsake.

There are many ways to incorporate hymns into your meditation: by singing them, by reflecting on them, or by humming them to Jesus in the way a parent hums to a child at bedtime. Whatever your offering, engage in it fully and God will accept it and be pleased.

Instrumental Music

If singing hymns isn't your thing, consider playing a little instrumental music to help with your time of meditation. Just be careful that the music you choose isn't too raucous. Instrumental renditions of our favorite hymns are great. So are some of our favorite songs from Christian artists, though we have to be careful of getting more into the music than getting into the Lord.

In general I would *not* recommend turning on the radio to meditate. You can't control the selections being played, and you might very well find yourself abandoning meditation time because the radio personalities keep interfering. Remember also that advertisements are played back much louder than music. The sound of someone busting into your prayer time to sell you something—or give you news, weather, and sports—will be incredibly distracting and off-putting. Best to leave the radio for the car.

It is important to not waste precious prayer time trying to find just the right piece of music to use. Choose your music well ahead of time—if you meditate in the morning, choose it the night before; if you meditate in the afternoon, choose it before lunch—so you can arrive settled and ready to go. (Preparing your musical selection before prayer also lends a feeling of seriousness to the whole thing; like you've got a date with the Holy Spirit and you're setting out your best clothes.)

Some people prefer to fly by the seat of their britches. They don't want to choose anything specific because they don't want to hem God in, so instead they turn their iPods to "shuffle." That's not bad if you can be sure that everything in your playlist is *appropriate*. It's one thing to have the machine sort through several different instrumental favorites, any of which enhance prayer; it's another for it to go from "There's Power in the Blood" to some bootie-shaking club song and then back again. The jolt will yank you out of prayer and you may not regain everything you lost.

Also beware of choosing music that is so peaceful and tranquil that you meditate yourself to sleep. If you can handle long stretches of quiet music, then fine, you have nothing to worry about. But if you can't, you might want to find music that "sways" a little, builds in intensity, dies away some, goes a little faster, goes a little slower, and so on. Find music that will keep you alert but not distracted.

A Note on New Age Music

Many of you are familiar with so-called New Age music—music that is used by New Agers and others for yoga, massage, meditation, and generating peaceful thoughts. You may wonder if using New Age music is permissible for Bible-believing Christians. It's a difficult but important question to answer.

My counsel is that you should use music that was created exclusively to glorify God, nothing else. While some of the New Age music sounds harmless, it is not harmless. Some New Age music invokes ancient gods and goddesses, or promotes beliefs that are completely contrary to Christianity, and it should be left alone. Which is not to say, if you do use it, that it will have any power over you; however, the use of non-Christian music will impede the your ability to access the presence of God.

It would do us well to remember Paul's advice to the Corinthians about meat sacrificed to idols—it's morally neutral. We know there are no gods out there receiving the meat, he says, so don't worry about it unless it bothers a brother or sister in Christ. In the same way, we know that a recording of ancient prayers to an Indian goddess can't hurt a believer who stands on the rock of faith. But we also don't want to play with fire. There are spiritual forces in the universe that are not obedient to the living God, and, while we don't need to fear them, we also don't need to invite them into our homes.

In general, if you see a CD advertising "nature sounds," "piano," or something else that sounds pretty innocent, it's probably fine. But look at the cover. Read the names of the pieces. Check to see who the artists are. Only then are you ready to make an informed decision. Be especially careful of any pieces where people sing in a language you do not understand. Gaelic is the ancient language of the Celts, and is increasingly being used for pagan rituals and witchcraft; Sanskrit is the holy language of Hinduism. The Tibetan language is used in the rites of Tibetan Buddhism. Native American music is often addressed to the Great Spirit or the Great Father, which Native American Christians understand to be the Holy Spirit or God the Father. Some tell the old stories of different tribes, and there's nothing wrong with listening to old stories. But if a person or a group is going to be singing praises to some other gods, that's not a CD I'd want to buy.

You don't need to be paranoid about this however. But do be careful when choosing music to use while meditating. Stick with music that was created to glorify our Father God which is in heaven; his name is Jesus.

Nature Sounds

Nature sounds — with or without musical accompaniment — are perfectly good for meditation. A recording of waves breaking on the shore, or rain falling in a forest glade, or the wind blowing through the trees, is conducive to prayer and meditation — especially when it puts you in mind of the Creator and his many mercies. Again, just be careful it doesn't lull you to sleep!

Self-Examination and Repentance

One of the hardest requirements of the Christian life is admitting — specifically and in detail — what we've done wrong or failed to do right. We try so hard to be good, to be nice, to be liked, but nobody, not a single one of us, is above the occasional hurtful or insensitive remark, blindness to the pain or gifts of others, judgmentalism instead of compassion, or a selfish decision that doesn't put others first. Sometimes these sins are deeply ingrained, and often appear as patterns or values instead of individual acts — and not only are those kinds of sins hard to admit to, they're hard to discern because they're so deeply rooted in our souls.

One use for meditation is to ask God to show us our sins and shortcomings so that we may repent and be healed. This is necessary, but it isn't easy. God is our loving Father and wants us to become the best disciples we can be, but it's never easy to hear criticism, even if we asked for it, and even if it's for our own good. It takes some true spiritual courage to ask an all-seeing Lord to shine light into the dark corners of our souls that we've kept hidden from ourselves — for good reason!

Many Christians dedicate a season to repentance, such as Lent, in order to spend time in self-examination leading to repentance. If your community doesn't observe a season like Lent, it's a good idea to set aside a regular discipline of self-examination and repentance. There are several ways to do this.

Set Aside a Time of the Year

Set aside a time of the year to dedicate to self-examination and repentance of sin. For some people this is the last week of the year, in preparation for a new beginning (one of God's great mercies!). Others choose the week or even the month before their birthday, another new beginning. If you are a parent, you could set aside some time leading up to Mother's Day or Father's Day to ask God to reveal your weaknesses and sins in your parenting; and for those who are married, the weeks leading up to your anniversary are a perfect time to pray that God shows you where you fall short and sin as a husband or wife.

Set Aside a Specific Day

Set aside a specific day within your regular meditation discipline for self-examination and repentance. If you meditate every day, perhaps one of those days on a regular basis could be given to inviting God to shine his light into your heart's dark corners. For many Christians, Friday is the traditional day of the week to focus on our sorrow for our sins. The most important thing is not what day we do it, but that we do it regularly.

Set Aside Time Every Day

It can be very good and beneficial to set aside time every day for self-examination and confession. I highly recommend you take time every day, especially before bedtime, to reflect on sins you committed that day. Admit your imperfections and ask God to forgive you so you will continue in his grace.

Daily self-examination and repentance of sin has the double blessing of getting right with God every day; so if tragedy strikes while you sleep, you (and your loved ones) know that you have confessed your sins and entrusted yourself to God's mercy. It also keeps the spiritual pipes from getting clogged up by sin and impeding an intimate relationship with the Lord. Lamentations 3:22–23 says, "Because of the Lord's great love we are not consumed, for his compassions never fail. They are new every morning; great is your faithfulness." Every believer should take comfort in this scripture because God gives us a clean slate daily, especially when we repent daily.

How to Meditate on Sin

In most ways, meditating on sin, or asking God to reveal our own sinfulness, is like meditating on any other area, subject, or focus. It involves regulated breathing, an open mind and seeking attitude, and a disciplined trust in God. It usually involves a verse from Scripture.[5] Breathe deeply, center yourself, and ask God to show you your sin as you meditate on his perfection and mercy, and your sorrow. Don't rush, don't make a laundry list of sins, just present yourself in all your imperfections and ask God to shine his light inside you. And when he does, ask him to help you do better in the future.

Wrestling with Angels and Demons

Do you remember the story of Jacob? Jacob had worked for his Uncle Laban for twenty years, married both of his daughters, and then left Laban in

---

5. See Appendix C for good verses to begin meditation

order to return to his homeland. He heard that his brother Esau was nearby, who had good reason to hate him, since Jacob had stolen his birthright twenty years before. He sent a message to Esau, hoping for reconciliation, and the messenger returned saying Esau was coming out with four hundred men. Jacob, afraid that Esau planned to destroy his family, sent them to the other side of the river while he waited for his brother's arrival.

Here's what happened next:

> That night Jacob got up and took his two wives, his two maidservants and his eleven sons and crossed the ford of the Jabbok. After he had sent them across the stream, he sent over all his possessions. So Jacob was left alone, and a man wrestled with him till daybreak. When the man saw that he could not overpower him, he touched the socket of Jacob's hip so that his hip was wrenched as he wrestled with the man. Then the man said, "Let me go, for it is daybreak."
>
> But Jacob replied, "I will not let you go unless you bless me."
>
> The man asked him, "What is your name?"
>
> "Jacob," he answered.
>
> Then the man said, "Your name will no longer be Jacob, but Israel, because you have struggled with God and with men and have overcome."
>
> Jacob said, "Please tell me your name."
>
> But he replied, "Why do you ask my name?" Then he blessed him there.
>
> So Jacob called the place Peniel, saying, "It is because I saw God face to face, and yet my life was spared."
>
> (Genesis 32:22–30)

It's interesting to consider that God's chosen people, the race from which Jesus came, was named "the one who struggles with God," after their father, Jacob, whom this man or angel renamed Israel. The spiritual world is full of forces that live either in obedience to God or in rebellion against him, and sometimes it's not easy to tell which is which. When the angel wounded Jacob's leg and left him with a lifelong limp, would Jacob have said he was godly or evil? But the wound was the doorway to the blessing, and all Jacob had to do was wrestle painfully with an angel in order to be blessed.

Test the Spirits

In our meditation, we have a perfect opportunity to follow John's injunction to "test the spirits" (1 John 4:1). When we are considering a choice or an action, we must meditate deeply on the Word of God and the nature of God, because we cannot trust our own judgment. As Jacob's story tells us, just because a course of action brings pain doesn't mean it's not from God. Obedience often leads to suffering, as the life of Jesus plainly shows us. And just because something brings us pleasure doesn't mean it's holy. Satan is a liar, and he disguises himself in bright, beautiful, and pleasant costumes in order to entice us. Fortunately, the stories of Jacob and Jesus, plus the writings of the New Testament, give us the tools to discern the spirits at work.

We know that an angel or obedient spirit will embrace and affirm the declaration, "Jesus is Lord." Paul tells us, "Therefore I tell you that no one who is speaking by the Spirit of God says, 'Jesus be cursed,' and no one can say, 'Jesus is Lord,' except by the Holy Spirit" (1 Corinthians 12:3). If you are meditating for guidance on whether forces in your life are angelic or demonic, use the gospel phrase "Jesus is Lord" as your mantra or repeated phrase. Repeating this declaration, the heart of the Christian gospel, will soon make anything unholy flee or fade under its power. Be careful though because some spirits are tenacious and need extensive prayer to be expelled. As with everything in the Christian life, a firm focus on the Word of God and Jesus as Lord will eventually defeat them.[6]

The next step in discerning the spirits trying to influence your life is to cast out harmful spirits in the name of Jesus Christ. Believe that you have this power; the Word of God has guaranteed it. We read it in Luke 10:17–20:

> The seventy-two returned with joy and said, "Lord, even the demons submit to us in your name."
>
> He replied, "I saw Satan fall like lightning from heaven. I have given you authority to trample on snakes and scorpions and to overcome all the power of the enemy; nothing will harm you. However, do not rejoice that the spirits submit to you, but rejoice that your names are written in heaven."

Command anything that does not confess Jesus as Lord or wishes harm to any of God's children to leave your mind and your home in the name of Jesus

---

6. If demonic spirits persist, seek Godly counsel from your pastor, spiritual leader, mature prayer warrior, etc. If you encounter demonic attacks during your time of meditation, call on Jesus until it lifts, but seek understanding and a defensive strategy against those attacks for the future.

Christ. It's not a bad idea to do this frequently; the enemy's servants are sneaky. Though they have to be invited in, they have ways of persuading you to do that. Look for them hiding in the dark corners of your life and throw them out!

I'm not talking about doing an exorcism here; true exorcisms are rarely needed and will take more prayer by members of the faith community. But I am talking about the demonic forces of culture, physical gratification, self-centeredness, and temptation. An idea can seem brilliant and exciting at the time, but in reality be a temptation cleverly disguised. The enemy can even use the church itself to lead you away. I once heard of a man who spent so much time at the church that he neglected his family and let his relationships fall apart. Obviously God didn't want that to happen, but the man didn't stop to discern the call to work for God inside the church building. And the enemy used his good intentions against him.

Battlefield of Prayer

Meditation can be used for more than discerning the spiritual influences in your life though. Sometimes the hour of meditation is the battlefield for a prayer warrior to wrestle with demons or angels, just as Jacob wrestled with an angel on the riverbank. Though you sit silently, breathing deeply in and out, to confront these messengers is a battle indeed, and you must be armed and prepared. Verses that declare the lordship of Jesus, the presence of the Holy Spirit, or the benevolent power of God the Father will serve you and protect you when you use them as your mantra, sword, and shield.

A demonic force in your life is anything that draws you further from God. Addiction is the name of one such demon. Others have names such as Pornography, Self-pity, Anxiety, Control, Lust, Insecurity, Need-to-Please, and Anger. And don't forget that they can disguise themselves. You might think you're being humble and virtuous when you say that God couldn't possibly love a lowly, messed up, sinful failure like you, but in the end that's just one more excuse not to commit. He said he loves you and you have to trust him more than you trust yourself. If you can't, or won't, that's a demon that has control of your heart. You have to face it down, fight it, and defeat it.

Angels and demons participate in our lives in ways we aren't always aware of, and even when we become aware of the spiritual forces around us, we can't be sure we know which is which. We must open ourselves to the revelation of God and the discerning power of the Holy Spirit, for only *he* can show us the truth of good and evil. We can only do that through meditation on the lordship of Jesus and the guidance of the Holy Spirit.

Chapter 12
Types of Meditation: Virtue, Fasting, and Meditational Walking

Meditating on Virtue

Virtues are habits of moral excellence and they make excellent topics of meditation. When we think of the sorts of attitudes we Christians should hone in on, we are generally thinking of the virtues.

Some people prefer other words over "virtue," like "integrity" and "character." Those are fine words because virtue *does* raise fundamental questions about personal integrity and the sort of character we wish to have. I will continue to use the word "virtue," however, because not only does it cover the entire field of desirable traits, but it can also be used when talking about particular virtues.

Christianity has always treated questions of virtue seriously. New life in Christ means a lot of things, including changing our habits of thought and action so they better reflect our adoption as sons and daughters of God. It should be no surprise then that we find several lists of virtues in the New Testament.

The traditional list of seven virtues comes down to us from the early church. These are the four *cardinal* virtues of ancient Greece (temperance, justice, courage, and prudence) and the three *theological* virtues listed by St. Paul in 1 Corinthians (faith, hope, and charity or love). Though this list is nowhere found in the Bible, all seven virtues are certainly held up for our consideration at different times. The story of Daniel in the lions' den, for example, is about faith and courage; the story of the good samaritan is about charity, and so on.

The list of seven virtues is obviously influenced by our Greco-Roman and Christian heritage, but the Bible itself contains several lists of virtues, all of which are desirable in a Christian. These include:

> **2 Corinthians 6:6–8:** Purity, understanding, patience and kindness;
>
> **Galatians 5:22–23:** Love, joy, peace, forbearance, kindness, goodness, faithfulness, gentleness, and self-control; and
>
> **Ephesians 4:32:** "Be kind and compassionate to one another, forgiving each other, just as in Christ God forgave you.[7]

---

7. Similar lists can be found in Ephesians 5:9; Philippians 4:8; Colossians 3:12; 1 Timothy 4:12 and 6:11; 2 Timothy 2:22 and 3:10; James 3:17; 1 Peter 3:8; and 2 Peter 1:5–7.

Meditating on virtue can take one of two forms: either meditating on God's attributes and then asking God to fill us with his Spirit, or meditating on the virtues themselves and asking God to give us instances when we can practice them. In either case we make it our practice to sit and place ourselves in God's presence, then read a relevant passage of Scripture, inviting the Spirit to open it up with all its implications.[8]

Paul tells us in his letter to the Philippians that "it is God who works in you to will and to act in order to his good purpose" (Philippians 2:13). If you pray for the Holy Spirit to help you to become a more virtuous person, then he will do that. But be aware, you're not going to become Christlike on your own. These aren't New Year's resolutions we're talking about. If you meditate on the virtues and ask God to make you a more virtuous person, he will put you smack dab in situations where you can exercise particular virtues. Virtues are honed through the choices we make; if you pray for patience, don't be surprised when God puts you behind a slow-moving truck on your way home from a long day at work. That's his way. And it will be up to you to make the choice to be patient and not honk and tailgate. Pray for virtue and then allow him to prompt you to make virtuous choices, and you'll find him making you more Christlike. As Paul tells the Corinthians, "And we, who with unveiled faces all reflect the Lord's glory, are being transformed into his likeness with ever-increasing glory, which comes from the Lord, who is the Spirit" (2 Corinthians 3:18).

Your meditation will be fruitful when you allow yourself to be guided by God. Pray for virtue, choose virtue, and you'll find yourself virtuous.

Meditation and Fasting

Meditation is a powerful spiritual discipline—but when it's joined with fasting, you've got spiritual dynamite on your hands! The Holy Spirit can change your life through fasting and prayer.

Scripture tells us that God hears the prayer of a man or woman fasting with a contrite heart. Fasting and prayer bring about revival: personal revival, yes, but also revival in our churches, revival in our cities, and revival in our country. The awesome power of the Holy Spirit will work through *you* as you meditate on the Scriptures and fast with a devout heart.

Unfortunately, fasting is one biblical practice neglected—*ignored* might be a better word—by most modern Christians. Even people who pride themselves

---

8. See Appendix A for attributes of God that you can meditate on.

on following God's Word to the letter will confess that they find religious fasting both morbid and strange.

And yet we'll fast before medical tests. We'll fast to lose weight. We'll fast to make ourselves outwardly beautiful. Why are we so reluctant to fast for the sake of the kingdom then? Maybe our reluctance stems from our not understanding what fasting actually is and how it's actually done.

Restrict the Amount of Food

Contrary to what most of us think, fasting does not necessarily mean you eat nothing at all. At its most basic, to fast is to *restrict the amount of food you take in*. Depending on the type of fast you're keeping, that might mean eating nothing, but it can also mean eating only one full meal a day, two-half meals, or even a bite every few hours.

The strictest fast is one in which nothing is eaten for a predetermined amount of time (usually twenty-four hours, but also two or three days, a whole week, or even forty days). Water and fruit juices are still consumed so the fast doesn't become debilitating; and medication, of course, must also be taken. I would suggest that a beginner fast strictly for only one day at a time; any longer than that and you risk hurting yourself. Pain is not the point of a fast and it isn't God's desire that you hurt yourself. Consult your physician if you feel called to a strict fast lasting longer than forty-eight hours.

Mitigated Fast

If you're new to fasting, consider starting off with a mitigated fast. In a mitigated fast you significantly *curtail* the amount of food you eat for a period of time, but you don't stop eating altogether.

A mitigated fast can be kept in one of several ways. One possibility is to eat a single full meal a day, with two smaller "bites" in place of the meals you're skipping. These bites are not snacks; they are meant to keep your energy up, to enable you to pray and to work. A piece of whole wheat toast with peanut butter and a handful of dried fruit on the side should be more than enough to keep you going. Drink plenty of water and juice throughout the day, just as you would in a strict fast. A mitigated fast is an especially good discipline if you have a history of medical problems, are under the age of sixteen, or over the age of sixty.

An easier form of the mitigated fast is to purposely forego a single meal—fasting through lunch, for example, and then breaking the fast with dinner. The very easiest mitigated fast is to take half portions at a meal — anyone can take one spoonful of corn or mashed potatoes instead of two.

Looked at as a restriction in the amount of food taken in, this is a spiritual discipline anyone can handle. If you feel yourself starting to swoon, or your blood sugar drops precipitously, by all means discontinue the fast. The point — let me say it again — is not to feel pain.

The Point of Fasting

So what is the point of fasting, if not to feel pain? The point is to purify our intentions and to learn, through our physical bodies, complete reliance upon God so our prayer is intensified.

So how does that work exactly? Let me give you an example.

I said earlier that you shouldn't attempt a strict fast right out of the gate, and that you should consult a doctor if you feel called to fast for more than forty-eight hours. Despite these warnings, however, many people — *Super-Christians* we might call them — will decide that God has called them to heroic fasting — forty days and forty nights kind of stuff. None of that mitigated fasting for them, nothing that requires a doctor's note. They want to do *real* fasting. They're going to show everybody how a *real* disciple fasts.

Do you see what's happening there? That person has made fasting a work of pride. "I am a *Super-Disciple*; therefore I will do the maximum allowed." Wake up. You're not Jesus. You're not Paul. You're a beginner. And just like any beginner, you need to take baby steps.

The first point of fasting is to purify our intentions. If you're fasting to prove to others how great a Christian you are, then your intentions are not pure. A fast like that is an abomination and it does you more spiritual harm than good.

The second point of a fast is to teach us, bodily, our complete reliance upon God. Undertaking a fast for which we are not prepared *might* help us learn reliance — but more likely it will fail and then we'll get depressed because we're not as great as we originally thought. We will not have learned the lesson fasting teaches. And if we do succeed in keeping the strict fast, then we'll be swelled up with pride, which is the opposite of reliance.

Fasting also intensifies prayer, which is the third point of fasting. You can't read the Bible long without running into that phrase, "fasting and prayer." They seem to go together. Fasting makes prayer more urgent. It cleans out the channels to the brain and it helps us think (and therefore pray) more clearly.

Fasting also *reminds* us to pray. Carry in your heart a verse from the Scriptures—an appropriate one might be, "My food is to do the will of him who sent me and to finish his work" (John 4:34), or "Do not work for food that spoils, but for food that endures to eternal life" (John 6:27)—and then, when your stomach growls or you become preoccupied with thoughts of food, calmly repeat the verse. Make it your prayer. Repeat it over and over in rhythm with your heartbeat until you begin to understand it from the inside out. And then, when the temptation subsides, continue your work until the next hunger pang.

Meditation on God's Word will be enhanced as you give yourself to fasting. Your mind will be clearer; you will have more energy to do God's will. And, most importantly, you will begin to trust God implicitly, knowing that he who provides food for the ravens when they cry will also feed you (Job 38:41). You will be hungry in body, yes, but your spirit will feel that it's being fed directly from the hand of God.

Walking Meditation

The last type of meditation we're going to discuss is walking meditation. *Walking* meditation? Isn't meditation done sitting down with your Bible in a quiet corner somewhere, eyes closed and legs crossed? Well, yes, that's certainly one method, but it's not the *only* method. Meditating on God's Word can be done in a variety of ways. The essential part of Christian meditation is pondering the Word of God in your heart; for some people that's going to mean sitting on the couch while for others it will mean something more active.

Anyone who has tried to meditate the traditional way knows it's often difficult to remain focused, alert, and awake. But in walking meditation we use the experience of walking as a way to slow ourselves down and remain aware of what we're thinking. We keep the awareness of our heart on a Scripture passage, but we also keep our bodies in motion, sometimes walking back and forth over a long path or even—if we're stuck inside—in a large circle around the living room rug.

You might doubt this is meditation, but let me assure you, it is. You may have already experienced something like it, when you've done the dishes or the laundry with a thought on your mind. You think of the problems of the day, or the remarks made by someone at work, and then you look down at the dishes, and they are done! You didn't even realize so much time had passed because you were deep in thought. We might call that "working meditation" or "action meditation," but it's the same principle.

Sitting meditation and walking meditation are obviously not exactly the same. You have to keep your eyes open during walking meditation, for example, or you might trip and fall. And be aware that people are more likely to talk to you in walking meditation because they'll think you're just wandering around the house or down the sidewalk. When those distractions come, allow them to come. Don't do violence to your reflections by pushing them out of your head; instead, let them gently recede for a moment while you deal with the person at hand. Then, when you're able, resume your walk and your meditation.

The basic principles are still there, however, whether you're sitting or walking: slowly and meditatively read a passage from the Scriptures. Let it sink in and then, when you feel ready, use the passage as a way of gazing lovingly upon the Lord. In sitting meditation you can simply let the passage lie open in your lap while you reflect on the Word of God; in walking meditation, holding it might be a distraction (or a hazard). My own suggestion is that you lay the Bible down or carry it behind your back. Keep it close, though, because the Lord may put it on your heart to go back to the text. The Bible is not dispensable to Christian meditation: it's the point of Christian meditation. If you can't meditate because you have trouble remembering what you've read, by all means open it up and look again.

The key to walking meditation is to slow down; not unnaturally slow, because you need to keep your balance and not be distracted by the act of walking itself, but the slow side of normal should do the trick. If you have time and space, time your steps with your heartbeat or your breath. To set a natural pace, stand still for fifteen or twenty seconds and take several slow, deep breaths. Then walk five or six feet and adjust your pace. Go as slowly as is comfortable and natural. Keep the pace steady, even if you pace back and forth over an area and must turn occasionally.

You can also match your breath and your words to the rhythm of your footsteps. For example, three breaths in plus three steps is a great way to establish a rhythm: in (step), in (step), in (step), out (step), out (step), out (step). Then you can easily recite words to that three-step rhythm:

- Lord — I — believe (in/step, in/step, in/step)
- Help — my — unbelief (out/step, out/step, out/step)

Or perhaps,

- You — are — the Messiah (in/step, in/step, in/step)
- The Son — of — God (out/step, out/step, out/step)

It doesn't have to be a three-step rhythm; here's a four-step one:

- To every — thing there — is a — season (in/step, in/step, in/step, in/step)
- And a time — to every — purpose — under heaven (out/step, out/step, out/step, out/step)

The trick is to keep your steps slow and steady, not allowing them to speed up. This is meditative walking, not power walking (though we might call it spiritual power walking!). You will find that intentionally pacing your body helps to slow down your mind. Walking meditation is perfect for those times when your mind is racing, your emotions are ramped up, you're too distracted to meditate while sitting down, or you're not sure what to do with all your pent-up energy.

Persevere in walking meditation and you will find that it can be done almost anywhere, at almost any time. Once you learn to slow yourself down, walk, and focus on the Word all at the same time, you will find yourself meditating while walking down supermarket aisles and mowing the lawn. You will find that you are more aware of your surroundings, not less, so there's no danger of knocking into other shoppers. You can even meditate on the Word as you walk down a crowded city sidewalk, surrounded by noise and people. The Word of God will dwell in you richly, right there in the middle of your everyday life.

There are so many ways to meditate that none of us will have an excuse not to begin. Meditation is so important for your Christian growth.

Section Three
Manifestation

Alas! I have nor hope nor health,
Nor peace within nor calm around,
Nor that content surpassing wealth
The sage in meditation found,
And walked with inward glory crowned.

—Percy Bysshe Shelley (1792–1822)

Chapter 13
Meditation's Physical Benefits

Who rises from prayer a better man, his prayer is answered.
—George Meredith, 1828–1909

What is Manifestation?

The first steps to embracing the power of meditation is to first *meditate*, which is encountering God's Word in a deep, focused, and living way; and the second is recitation, saying with your lips what God has done in your life. As we said earlier—it's the *seeing* and the *saying*—approaching the power and proclaiming the power. But that is not all there is to it. There's one more step. It's where the rubber meets the road of the spiritual life; it's the *being* of the Christian life. We call it "manifestation."

Meditation becomes manifestation when you can start to see it working out in your day-to-day life. This happens in a lot of ways, which we'll talk about in this section. But for every way *seeing* becomes *being*, God's power and love are manifested, made real, made a part of your life, and deeply engrained in the fabric of your existence.

Physical Benefits

Like so many things God tells us to do, the benefits of meditation are far-reaching. Yes, we want to meditate on the Word so we can get closer to God, but that increased spiritual relationship isn't the only thing we get out of it. God is so good that he makes something he commands *good* for every level of our life! The way God has arranged it, meditation is good for our bodies, minds, emotions, and relationships, as well as for our spirits.

Effects of Stress

Earlier in this book we talked about the effects of stress. Stress is what happens when your brain and body prepare themselves for battle—only you're not going into battle; you're just going to work, school, or to a church meeting. But your body doesn't know the difference because of the amount of stress you're under. Every cell in your body is getting ready to pick up a sword and fight for your life. Here's what happens to your body when you're under stress:

Your body produces more of a hormone called cortisol. Cortisol is like the general calling the rest of your body's systems to arms; it triggers all the other stress responses. A little bit of cortisol in the bloodstream, even at higher short-term levels, can be good for you; it's responsible for that great feeling of anticipation and readiness you get right before a game, and the focus and energy you feel while you're playing. It kicks into gear when you see your little one waddling toward the street, signaling for the oxygen and adrenaline you need to sprint after him. God gave us all these reactions for our good, right? But if you're always stressed, and your cortisol levels are always high, your body will respond with some pretty bad reactions. A lot of the ones listed below come from the call-to-arms sent out by a flood of cortisol.

Your body reprioritizes its use of resources and starts pulling blood away from your organs and limbs so that it can go to your heart, lungs, and brain — the ones needed most for immediate survival. This is supposed to be a temporary thing, but if it continues, it means you don't get the blood (which carries the oxygen) to other vital organs like your liver, kidneys, stomach, bowels, hands, and feet — not as much as they need anyway.

Your immune system crashes for a while because your body isn't as worried about catching a cold as it is about surviving the next few hours (at least, your body thinks it's going to be a couple of hours). As a result, you may find that you're always sick or coming down with something.

Your pancreas floods your system with sugar because sugar gives your cells the extra energy they need to fight. Because of this reaction, stress is a major contributor to diabetes. And for diabetics and others with health issues, stress can be a life-or-death issue.

Your heart rate picks up speed, forcing blood through vessels that might not be able to handle the extra work. Blood pressure spikes, sometimes staying there, pushing way too much blood too fast through your blood vessels, putting your life in danger. Stress is a major factor in heart disease, heart attacks, and strokes.

Your thinking may become fuzzy, or it may accelerate to a mile a minute until your thoughts overwhelm you. It's not a coincidence that people in high-stress occupations often self-medicate with legal or illegal drugs, abuse alcohol, are violent with their families, have nervous breakdowns, or commit suicide. Stress can lead to all these outcomes because people's thoughts become out of control, overwhelming, and have no way to handle them.

Your thyroid gets suppressed, which means your metabolism gets out of whack and you don't get calcium to your bones. You become weak, confused, and lethargic. Your body can't do basic things like convert food into energy, and you may gain weight—which can lead to depression, heart disease, diabetes. Are you beginning to see what a vicious cycle this is?

Your bones become more brittle and break more easily. Because of the effects on the thyroid just mentioned, stress leeches calcium from your bones, making them weaker. A healthy, calm body gets all of its nutrients where they need to go, but a body that thinks it's under attack diverts all of its nutrients to places they don't belong—like your heart. While your bones are becoming more brittle from lack of calcium, that calcium gets deposited in your heart and lungs, blocking the way for important functions.

Your muscles start to weaken and decrease. You would think that if your body thought it was always swinging a sword your muscles would get stronger, but actually the opposite happens. Any body builder can tell you that your muscles do not strengthen during the actual workout—they strengthen during the rest periods between sets. And if your muscles are always tensed and never get to rest, they never get to strengthen. They gradually lose strength, making you physically weaker.

Your body takes its focus away from its natural healing processes (it's in battle, remember? The time for healing is later—if later ever comes). Wounds and injuries heal slowly, and colds and other illnesses seem to linger for months.

Your body starts to hoard abdominal fat, which keeps your organs from working properly and puts you at higher risk for heart attack and stroke.

You start to crave sweet or salty foods because your body is trying to replenish the sugar-energy and water the constant battle conditions are depleting from it.

You gain weight, increasing your risk for heart disease, diabetes, cancer ,and depression.

And you lose sleep, increasing your risk for irritability, heart disease, stroke, diabetes, depression, anxiety, and impaired judgment, and making you a danger on the road or around heavy machinery.

After a battle you're supposed to return to a state of balance, where all your systems return to their natural place and any necessary healing can begin. But when there's too much stress in your life, the battle never ends, and you don't get the time for healing your body needs.

There are some things in your life that you can't change. It would be nice to get a less stressful job, or to have fewer papers due at the end of the semester, or to live in a world where everyone was nice and nobody made you angry or anxious. It would be wonderful to live in a place where we had all our bills paid and we didn't have to worry about having too much month at the end of the money. But that would probably be heaven, and all those things still have to be dealt with in this life. But meditation can help.

Meditation Helps

Here's how meditation can help. You can't change the things outside of yourself, but there are things you can change inside yourself, even some of those involuntary reactions like blood pressure and the cortisol rush. Stress is a reaction from inside you, and meditation can relieve stress. Meditation can take you out of the battle, even if it's only for a few minutes.

Meditation forces you to calm down and to breathe deeply. Remember that simple, beginners' exercise we did earlier, where you just sat and counted your breaths? Just that one easy step brought calm to your body and mind, and it brought health — in the form of oxygen — to every cell in your body. And that was before you even brought the Word of God or the Holy Spirit into it. Stress causes us to breathe shallowly and to tense our upper body muscles, keeping our lungs from getting the full amount of air that we need. But the simple, meditative act of deep breathing can relax our muscles, getting rid of those knots and aches, thus reducing the flood of cortisol racing through our system.

Another great way meditation can help is that the effects last a lot longer than just the moments you spend actually meditating. Once your breathing slows and deepens, your blood pressure drops, your heart stops beating so fast, your muscles relax, and your head clears, it all tends to stay that way for the next few hours. A few minutes of meditation can have hours of results. The more often you meditate, the longer-lasting the results are, and the less stress there will be in your life.

Body-Benefits

Here are some of the body-benefits of regular meditation:

Pain Control

The American Cancer Society is one of many groups that recommends meditation as a form of pain control. Our immune system needs oxygen in order to fight and heal—what they don't need is cortisol calling all of our battle responses to action. Meditating involves the deep breathing techniques that bring oxygen to all our cells, helping reduce the pain response and increase our cells' ability to heal. For a Christian, meditation for pain control can involve a focus on Jesus the Healer, and the envisioning of his gentle touch. Studies have shown that regular meditation can reduce chronic pain and the anxiety and fear that come with it.

While we meditate primarily to commune with the Lord, studies suggest that it's also effective in relieving pain. In controlling your breath and relaxing your body, you make it possible to "pray through the pain" and improve your quality of life. Many people report spending some time in meditation while recuperating from surgery and finding their pain significantly lessened. That's because it helps focus the mind on other thoughts, other feelings, and away from the pain and stress of the current situation. Pain causes anxiety and elevates blood pressure. Meditation, however, is proven to calm the nerves and bring down blood pressure.

"There's no doubt from the standpoint of research and my own clinical experience," says Dr. Stan Chapman, a pain treatment expert, "that meditation can reduce both the experience of pain and help people manage stress resulting from having pain. Meditation is a therapy offered in all comprehensive pain centers."[9]

Physical pain also takes a toll on our mental state, and, in meditating on the words of Scripture, we can change our thoughts and therefore our reaction to the pain. While meditation won't deal with the cause of the pain, it can help diminish the sensations, opening every area of our life to God's healing power.

One believer said, "When I had plantar fasciitis and had to have shots in my heel, I used deep breathing and meditation to put my mind in another place so I didn't feel the pain. The physician assistant was surprised by how well that worked." She still had to have the treatment, but her ability to meditate helped her get through the treatment with a minimal amount of pain.

---

9. WebMD, http://www.webmd.com/balance/guide/transcendental-meditation

Reduction in Headaches

There is evidence that regular meditation not only controls pain, but can keep headaches from happening at all. Headaches, like a lot of pain, are actually a gift to the human body, the body's way of warning the brain that something isn't right and you better pay attention. But all too often, instead of treating the real problem—which is frequently stress—we just medicate it and cover up the symptoms. Many people who struggle with migraines don't find medication helpful since it often has bad side effects and comes in high doses. Headache medication can also suppress the headache, only to have it come rebounding back when the medicine wears off. But with regular meditation, blood vessels don't constrict as much, since they are getting the oxygen they need to conduct blood where it needs to go. With regular meditation, the rapid heartbeat, shallow breathing, and flood of cortisol that comes with stress are reduced, and the defensive reaction of your body calms down. Things are set right, so the body's painful warning system doesn't have to kick into gear, and headaches go away.

Improved Immune System

Studies show that consistent meditation improves overall health, especially the working of the immune system. In one study, patients with immune disorders such as HIV found their CD4 cells—basic building blocks of the immune response—increasing after a short discipline of regular meditation. This isn't a psychosomatic reaction—it's not just that you feel better because you think you will or you think you should. There is a measurable physiological reaction taking place in the body after a course of focused and consistent meditation.

The body becomes stronger and calmer, able to deal better with stress, and therefore able to turn its attention to battling intruders such as germs, viruses, and bacteria, things it could seldom turn its attention to when operating under the battle conditions of stress. When life is taken out of the battle, which happens through meditation, the body can work to keep it healthy on a day-to-day level.

You've probably noticed that people who live stressful lives tend to have more than their share of allergies and colds, and tend to catch every illness that makes its way through the school or office. And when they do, those illnesses usually hit them harder than they hit other people. That's because those stressed bodies have no time to deal with these inconvenient illnesses—they are in the middle of a battle. You wouldn't stop fighting in the middle of a war, set down your sword, and deal with some minor discomfort. You'd be killed. But that's what your body thinks is going on, so it can't deal with something minor like a cold or the flu. But if you can calm your bodily systems down, your immune system can again pay attention to the comparatively less serious threats — and keep them from becoming major ones.

This isn't just theoretical. Study after study shows that even just a few weeks of meditation can increase your body's ability to fight disease and illness. Scientists and doctors aren't sure why this should be the case — the phrase they use for this is "the mechanism for this result is unclear." But believers know that we have a God who wants the best for us — spirit, mind, and body — and he makes it so that following his will is good for us in every sense. Only God can see the big picture for our lives, including our bodies. And he has created us to thrive when we live in obedience to him and intimacy with him. Meditation with the Word of God brings health in every sense.

Lowered Blood Pressure

There's a story on a popular medical website about a man who lived a very stressful life. He started experiencing chest pains, so he went to the emergency room, thinking he was having a heart attack. He wasn't; he was diagnosed with Gastric Esophageal Reflux Disorder (GERD), a severe form of acid reflux (more on this disorder later!). But he learned that he was at high risk for having a heart attack, it was just a matter of time, since his blood pressure was through the roof. On the advice of a friend, this man started meditating twenty minutes a day, and within a month his blood pressure had returned to normal.

Blood pressure simply refers to the amount of resistance to blood flow in your blood vessels. If they are clear, clean, and healthy, blood flows smoothly through them at exactly the right rate. Your heart works at a normal healthy pace, and everything functions as it should. But if your arteries start to get clogged, from plaque and other materials building up on the inner arterial walls, the same amount of blood still has to get through, but there's less room for it to pass. Your heart has to work a lot harder to push it through, and the amount of pressure in your blood vessels increases. That much pressure can put a lot of strain on the heart and vessels, leading to ruptures — heart attacks, aneurysms, and strokes. As we know, those ruptures can be dangerous and deadly.

Anyone is susceptible to high blood pressure since it's a normal reaction to these unhealthy conditions. But some people are at an even higher risk, and if you're one of them, meditation is not just advisable, but an urgent necessity. If you have one of the following characteristics, taken from WebMD, you might have more of a risk for high blood pressure:

- Age. Older people have a higher risk of high blood pressure.
- Race. African-Americans have a higher risk of high blood pressure.
- Family history.
- Being overweight or obese.
- Not being physically active.
- Using tobacco.
- Too much salt (sodium) in your diet.
- Too little potassium in your diet.
- Too little vitamin D in your diet.
- Drinking too much alcohol.
- Stress.

How can meditation help with high blood pressure? The most important thing meditation can do is to slow down the heart rate and increase the intake of oxygen. Blood flows for the purpose of getting oxygen to every cell in the body; the more your heart beats and the more your stress level increases, the less oxygen is being carried with every breath. But if you're breathing deeper, as you do in meditation, you're supplying more oxygen to each heartbeat—full of blood. More oxygen reaches every cell just because you're breathing as your body was designed to do.

The other thing that meditation does is to slow down your heart rate. It reminds your body that this is a time of rest, not battle, and allows your heart to return to its healthy resting rate—something it rarely does if you're under stress. And, of course, we have heard what Bishop Augustine has told us about our hearts and Christian meditation: "Our hearts are restless, Lord, until they rest in thee." Don't spiritualize this too much; our hearts literally rest when we meditate on the Word of God. And a rested, calm, slowly-beating heart, carrying blood cells packed with oxygen, is a heart that guides the body into lower blood pressure, and lowers our risk for ruptures, attacks, and death.

Certain Chronic Conditions

These might include sleep apnea, kidney disease, and even pregnancy.

Heart Disease

According to a study presented at a conference of the American Heart Association in 2009, [10] people who practice meditation have a remarkably reduced rate of heart disease and all its complications—around fifty percent lower! This was over and above a control group which was given techniques such as diet, exercise, and health education. Those things are important, but nothing had so much of an effect on heart disease as meditation did.

The study is especially important because the subjects were two hundred and one African-American men, a group that is at high risk for stress, diabetes, stroke, and heart disease. It shows that even in a high risk group, where people are likely to get this serious disease at some point in their lives, meditation can fight against that internal enemy. Your genes are not your destiny and your ethnic group is not your fate. Just by following God's command to meditate, you can start to heal your heart.

Part of the reason meditation works so well—other than the fact that God set it up that way—was discussed in the previous section about blood pressure. High blood pressure is a major contributor to heart disease, so anything you can do to keep your blood pressure low and stable will be good for your heart. Another important factor is stress relief—there's hardly an illness in your body that doesn't stem at least in part from stress, and meditation helps deal with that stress. Remember, if your heart always thinks it's in battle, it's going to beat hard and fast all the time, forcing blood out at a rate it can't keep up with. It will wear out on you if you don't let it rest and relax.

Not only can meditation improve your blood pressure and heart disease, it's also good for other heart ailments. For example, a 2007 study showed that meditation can be beneficial to people suffering from congestive heart failure too.

Diabetes

We've already discussed that one of the chief stress responses is that the pancreas starts pumping more sugar into the blood. Again, this is both a good and godly response—there's no need to blame the pancreas for doing its job! If you really were in battle, the way your body thinks you are, you would need all that extra sugar to feed your cells and give you energy for the fight. It's not easy to keep up that energy level, and your pancreas is trying to give you what you need.

But when your body isn't actually in a fight, that flood of sugar into the bloodstream can be dangerous. If you're not already diabetic, it's the fastest route to becoming it. If you are diabetic, stress can spike your blood glucose

---

10. Reported in this article: http://www.telegraph.co.uk/health/healthnews/6581495/Meditation-cuts-risk-of-heart-attack-by-half.html.

levels faster than a piece of birthday cake. Many people find that they are not able to get their BSGs under control, no matter how carefully they eat or how diligently they exercise, until they can get their stress levels under control. And as we have seen, one of God's great gifts of meditation on his Word is to help us control those stress levels.

Irritable Bowel Syndrome

When your body is tense, even the most internal of organs clench up, causing painful cramps and other problems. One such syndrome is Irritable Bowel Syndrome, also known as IBS. It is a painful, inconvenient, and sometimes embarrassing collection of symptoms that up to twenty percent of the population suffers from. The symptoms can include bloating, flatulence, cramps, and diarrhea. A well-known study [11] conducted in 2001 attempted to discern whether meditation would be a legitimate treatment for IBS. The result was that a group that meditated twice a day, for fifteen minutes a day, recorded their symptoms lessening significantly within two weeks, and sometimes disappearing altogether within six weeks. Since then, IBS groups such as IBS-Life and Help for IBS, have endorsed it for anyone suffering from IBS. Since God made our bodies the way they are, even down to our digestive systems, it makes sense that he'd provide a way to keep them healthy and working right.

Women's Health

There are things you sisters out there have to deal with, things that cause you stress, that we men can't really understand. But the Lord can, and he has arranged it so that meditation can help you in those areas too. For example, ladies, if you struggle with PMS (premenstrual syndrome), meditation can help with that. Women who meditate find that their hormones settle down and balance out, their physical symptoms aren't as bad, and their irritability and fatigue are more controllable and less severe. One study showed that for women who meditate, there was a fifty-eight percent decrease in PMS symptoms alone.

Meditation has also proven helpful in two ways to women who are experiencing infertility problems. Meditation can help women by helping reduce the amount of stress, anxiety, depression, fatigue, and grief that they feel, and making them more able to feel those natural emotions without being overwhelmed. According to one study, about thirty-five percent of those meditating women became pregnant within six months of beginning their meditation discipline.

---

11. http://www.ncbi.nlm.nih.gov/pubmed/11419611?dopt=Abstract

Nursing mothers who meditate are able to keep a healthy flow of milk, even doubling their milk production, and menopausal women who meditate have fewer and less intense hot flashes and other symptoms. The daughters of God have the special ministry of sharing on God's creation, and he wants his ladies to be healthy and happy when they do it. Meditation on his Word and deepening your love relationship with him, is the best way to share God's creative power in the way he intended.

Asthma

Studies suggest that meditation can help with asthma, from decreasing the frequency of attacks to lessening their severity. Meditation relaxes our mind and body, which makes it easier to control our emotions. When we're calm, our blood pressure goes down and the flow of blood and oxygen to our heart and brain increases, which cuts down on the likelihood of an asthmatic attack. Breathing steadily, when practiced every day, also strengthens our lungs and airways.

Breathing techniques learned in meditation can also be used during an attack, in order to stay calm. Concentration on breath and heartbeat helps a person relax, and an appropriate phrase from Scripture—for example, "Let everything that has breath praise the Lord" (Psalm 150:6)—can provide a godly focus as well as a cry for help.

By meditating on the Word of God for fifteen to thirty minutes every day, an asthmatic may find that his attacks are less severe, that they occur less frequently, and that they are easier to manage.

As you can see, there are tremendous benefits to meditating on God's Word. Not only spiritual benefits, but many bodily benefits as well. All the effects of stress from our normal day-to-day living can be decreased by giving ourselves to meditation on God and his Word.

Chapter 14

The Psychological, Relational, and Spiritual Benefits of Meditation

Good for Our Minds

Meditation can be thought of as a spiritual and mental exercise. It's not easy at first, but the more you exercise, the better at it you become. Just like physical exercise trains the body to be stronger, faster, and have more endurance, consistent meditation trains the mind, disciplines it, and makes it work better, harder, and faster.

Meditation is intended to help us draw our minds away from the constant preoccupation we have with our worldly concerns. It trains them to think about spiritual realities; and when we have a better grasp of these, we can better deal with the situations of the world.

Meditation literally makes people smarter. Studies have shown that people who meditate have "significantly greater brain activity, called gamma wave activity, in areas associated with learning and happiness, compared with those who didn't practice meditation…"[12]

Not only that, but meditation can also improve your concentration. It's like a concentration workout for your mind, since during meditation you have to train your attention to focus, to stop wandering, and to come back, time and time again, to the verse, story, image, or prayer at hand. Once you work out those concentration muscles through meditation, it's so much easier to flex them in your day-to-day life and work.

Psychological and Behavioral Problems

Life is difficult when you suffer from psychological and behavioral problems, such as anxiety, bipolar disorder, depression, and Post Traumatic Stress Disorder (PTSD). Doctors sometimes prescribe medication to help with these problems, but meditation on the Word of God can also be of help. Meditation not only puts us in contact with the Spirit of God, but it also changes our mood, which, in turn, changes our thoughts and our resulting behavior.

---

12. "Meditation Balances the Body"s Systems," by Jeane Lerche Davis. WebMD, http://www.webmd.com/balance/guide/transcendental-meditation.

While most studies on the benefits of meditation are not referring specifically to Christian meditation, they are nearly unanimous in saying that a few moments of silence and meditation every day benefit the body and mind. It calms a person down, provides a quiet space for reflection, and affects his or her mood. A nine-year-long study at the University of Michigan, for example, found that people who meditated regularly reported feeling happier, better able to manage stress, and fought less with their peers.

We should not forgo medical help for medical problems. But meditation in conjunction with whatever else your doctor prescribes can be quite beneficial. Our body and mind can benefit from regular, heartfelt communication with the Lord Jesus. And there is no better way to connect with him in a deep way than through meditation.

Good for Our Emotions

People don't feel well these days, and it's not just in their bodies. We're worried, afraid, angry, frustrated, insecure, and even desperate. There's so much to deal with, and we often don't feel like we can handle everything thrown at us. If you add in the chemical imbalances so many people struggle with, it's often hard just to be happy.

But study after study shows that meditation can bring relief to those suffering from any form of mental illness or distress. For example, people with depression do far better in their current treatment plans when meditation is added to their routines. In some cases, they are able to get off medication altogether and manage their condition through meditation and exercise. Many have to stay on medication, however, but often it's only a minimal amount and they don't have to increase it as often as they once did.

The same is true for anxiety, which is a response to stress that we all have. Obviously, if you reduce stress, you'll reduce the anxiety response to it. A lot of people are so anxious that they are on medication for their anxiety, just so they can get through their day without being overwhelmed with worry. But a lot of studies show that meditation reduces anxiety every bit as well as medication does. Remember, your body thinks you're in battle, and it's pretty smart to be anxious about your life in the middle of a battle. But everyday life isn't really that kind of battle, and battle-anxiety isn't helpful from day to day. Meditation can relieve that kind of stress and anxiety, making you feel better.

If you're a Christian and struggling with anxiety, try to spend some time every day meditating on the promises of Jesus. Here is a really good one to begin with; Jesus exhorting us to be free from anxiety.

> Therefore I tell you, do not worry about your life, what you will eat or drink; or about your body, what you will wear. Is not life more important than food, and the body more important than clothes? Look at the birds of the air; they do not sow or reap or store away in barns, and yet your heavenly Father feeds them. Are you not much more valuable than they? Who of you by worrying can add a single hour to his life?
>
> And why do you worry about clothes? See how the lilies of the field grow. They do not labor or spin. Yet I tell you that not even Solomon in all his splendor was dressed like one of these. If that is how God clothes the grass of the field, which is here today and tomorrow is thrown into the fire, will he not much more clothe you, O you of little faith? So do not worry, saying, "What shall we eat?" or "What shall we drink?" or "What shall we wear?" For the pagans run after all these things, and your heavenly Father knows that you need them. But seek first his kingdom and his righteousness, and all these things will be given to you as well. Therefore do not worry about tomorrow, for tomorrow will worry about itself. Each day has enough trouble of its own. (Matthew 6:25–34)

Since we've seen that just the act of meditation reduces anxiety, the act of meditating on Jesus' promises will reduce it twofold. Medication is a wonderful resource and a gift from God, but sometimes we forget to look first to the gifts that God has already built into the body, and meditation helps us access those built-in gifts.

One of the great benefits of meditation is that it helps us let go. We get so close to our problems, needs, and tasks, but meditation focuses our brain in a completely different direction — on the big picture, on God's vision of things. When we have a God's-eye-view, which we can get from immersing ourselves in his Word, the little things don't upset us as much. We can let the little things go, keeping ourselves calm, while spending our energy on what's important.

Good for Our Relationships

Empathy is the human capacity to be affected by others' feelings. It's what's going on when we say to someone, "I'm so happy for you," or "I hate that," or "I've been there, and here's what helped me." When people experience an emotion—happiness, amusement, fear, dejection, sorrow—they have a certain reaction in their brains. Chemicals kick in and synapses start connecting all over the place. It turns out that if someone is sharing an experience empathetically with another person, they have almost the same reaction in their brains as well. If someone is happy and shares his good news with you, your happy-for-him response will look just like his happy response when they're mapped out in the brain.

That means that there's a physiological, as well as an emotional, basis for empathy. And we've seen that meditation can have a strong effect on our physiological functions. Studies done by the National Institute for Health show that compassion meditation actually increases the empathetic reaction that people have. The more you meditate, and the more time you spend in meditation, the more you care about how other people feel.

Obviously, the more we care about others' feelings, the better our relationships are going to be. Think about all those times when you've felt really stressed, and someone you care about came to you with a problem. Instead of responding empathetically, we often say something like, "I have my own problems right now—I just can't deal with yours on top of them!" But when we meditate and reduce our stress, not only do we have the time and resources to deal with someone else's problems, but we truly do care more about them.

Compassion meditation is actually a Buddhist technique, but it can easily be adjusted for Christians—because we know that Jesus is the embodiment of the Father's compassion. Buddhists meditate on the quality of compassion itself, trying to become aware of it in themselves and others. Christians should start their compassion meditation by focusing on the compassion of Jesus toward others. Some good Bible verses for starting out with Christian compassion meditation include:

> A man with leprosy came to him and begged him on his knees, "If you are willing, you can make me clean."
>
> Filled with compassion, Jesus reached out his hand and touched the man. "I am willing," he said. "Be clean!" (Mark 1:40–41)

> He said to her, "Daughter, your faith has healed you. Go in peace and be freed from your suffering" (Mark 5:34)
>
> I have compassion for these people; they have already been with me three days and have nothing to eat. If I send them home hungry, they will collapse on the way, because some of them have come a long distance. (Mark 8:2–3)
>
> But love your enemies, do good to them, and lend to them without expecting to get anything back. Then your reward will be great, and you will be sons of the Most High, because he is kind to the ungrateful and wicked. Be merciful, just as your Father is merciful. (Luke 6:35–36)
>
> Do not be afraid, little flock, for your Father has been pleased to give you the kingdom. (Luke 12:32)

Another relationship benefit of meditation is that you gain patience, both with yourself and with others. Through deep breathing and calm, focused thinking, you're able to stop and consider before you react to something. When you're able to do that, you are less likely to snap at someone, and more likely to think through the best things to say or do, even in difficult situations. You'll listen much better to others because your mind and heart have been in training to listen to the Word of God.

Spiritual Benefits of Meditation

The most important benefits of meditation have to do with our souls, and the ever-deepening relationship with God we cultivate through meditating on his Word every day. That relationship is deepened in several important ways. I want to discuss some of the spiritual benefits of meditation.

A Deeper Knowledge of Scripture

As we listen for the voice of the Lord in meditation, we may find that we are gaining a deeper knowledge of God's Holy Word. The goal of meditation is intimacy with God, of course, not memorization. But we can't help but become more familiar with the Bible when we use it as the basis of our meditation and prayer.

In fact, it's not just deeper knowledge we acquire, it's also the ability to apply the knowledge we've gained to certain situations. Think about it: the more we meditate on the Scriptures, the better we know them; the better we know them, the better equipped we are to use them in our daily life. We will find that the application of biblical truths comes more easily when we meditate regularly because we are daily immersing ourselves in biblical words and phrases.

You'll be amazed the first time you sit at the kitchen window, watching the rain come down, and hear within you these words from the book of Isaiah:

> As the rain and the snow come down from heaven, and do not return to it without watering the earth and making it bud and flourish, so that it yields seed for the sower and bread for the eater, so is my word that goes out from my mouth: It will not return to me empty, but will accomplish what I desire and achieve the purpose for which I sent it. (55:10–11)

Your perspective will change as you experience something like this, and you will know in your heart that the Spirit rains down his blessings upon men and women to bring forth fruits worthy of himself.

Love is Proportioned to Knowledge

We know all too little about the Bible. In fact, if we memorized every verse from beginning to end, we still would know too little about it. That's because the Bible is the expression of God's thought, his written communication to humanity. God's thought is inexhaustible, so there's always more to learn. But our love of something is proportioned to the knowledge we have of it. I can't truly love someone about whom I know no absolutely nothing. I would at least have to know they existed in order to love them, and even then I would probably want to know a great deal more before I was prepared to say I loved them.

We say we love God, but how well do we actually know him? What do we really know about him? Here we have a Book—a collection of divinely-inspired texts—from which we can learn as much about God as it is humanly possible to know, but we seldom take the time to read it. It sits on a shelf from Monday to Saturday, comes down on Sunday morning, then goes right back up on Sunday night. But our love is proportioned to our knowledge. The more we know about something or someone, the more there is to love. Why leave the Bible on the shelf when you can open it up every day, meditate on God's Word, and gain a deeper knowledge of him? If we truly love him, we'll want to learn more about him.

One of the benefits to meditation, then, is the greater familiarity we get of the Bible. And as our knowledge of Scripture grows, so does our love for God.

Ignorance of Scripture is Ignorance of God

If it's true that knowledge of Scripture is knowledge of God, then it's also true that ignorance of Scripture is ignorance of God. (That's not my own observation; it belongs to Jerome, a great biblical scholar who lived in the Holy Land in the fifth century.) In other words, Bible study is not an optional luxury for the Christian. It's essential. If you don't know the Scriptures, then you don't know the God revealed in those Scriptures.

Jerome said something else in reference to the Bible: "Love the Holy Scriptures and wisdom will love you. Love wisdom and she will keep you safe." What a great observation! God's Word is his wisdom. Since Jesus is both the Word and Wisdom of God the Father, then loving God's Word in the Bible translates into loving God's Word, who is Jesus. In other words, love the Bible and Jesus will keep you safe. The more we immerse ourselves in the Bible through the disciplines of meditation and prayer, the more of God's protective armor covers us.

And that armor, in the form of a deeper familiarity with and understanding of Scripture, will be sufficient for repelling any number of spiritual attacks. For example, if the devil tempts you to despair, you can shout with the multitudes in the book of Revelation: "You are worthy, our Lord and God, to receive glory and honor and power, for you created all things, and by your will they were created and have their being" (4:11).

If he tempts you to pride, you can say to yourself, "For dust you are and to dust you will return" (Genesis 3:19).

If the devil provokes lust within you, you can repel him with Matthew 5:28: "But I tell you that anyone who looks at a woman lustfully has already committed adultery with her in his heart" (Ladies, you can turn that around without damaging the meaning of Jesus' words: "Anyone who looks at a man lustfully has already committed adultery with him in her heart." The point is not that a man does this, but that we all commit adultery in our heart when we give into lustful thoughts.)

Ignorance of Scripture is indeed ignorance of God. But it also leaves us defenseless when our enemy prowls around like a roaring lion (1 Peter 5:8).

We will gain a deeper understanding of the Bible as we use it in meditation. But don't hear me saying that we learn more facts as we read Scripture; we will learn more facts, but there's still a deeper benefit, which is that we will come to love God better, know God's ways from the inside out, and be given the gift of wisdom to know how to apply it in every situation.

The Fruits of the Holy Spirit

When a tree gets water, good soil, and plenty of sun, it produces good fruit. Its fruit will be sweet to the taste, and it will feed and refresh people. Just like that, the Christian whose life is nourished with prayer and fellowship with God will produce fruits of the Spirit. And like the fruit from a fruit tree, those fruits of the Spirit will feed and refresh, not only the Christian, but all with whom the Christian comes into contact.

Where the Spirit is, we find an abundant orchard of spiritual fruits. But while many are familiar with the gifts of the Spirit, not everyone is familiar with the Spirit's fruits. The gifts of the Spirit and the fruits of the Spirit are not the same things. The gifts of the Spirit—like any gifts—come from outside us, from a Giver. A gift is not something you earn; it's something the giver bestows upon you for some reason. The gifts of the Spirit are bestowed upon the Christian, for reasons known only to the Giver himself, who is God.

The fruits of the Spirit, on the other hand, are grown, not given. Like any fruit, they are the result of the inner principle of life brought forth through constant nurturance. The Spirit is the ultimate cause of the growth, but it's important to note that the fruit comes from something working inside of you. They are the result of growing "in the grace" (2 Peter 3:18).

Paul Describes the Fruits of the Spirit

Paul lists the fruits of the Spirit in several places. In the letter to the Galatians, he writes, "But the fruit of the Spirit is love, joy, peace, patience, kindness, goodness, faithfulness, gentleness and self-control. Against such things there is no law." (5:22–23a).

He also gives us a list of fruits in his letter to the Colossians, when he counsels us:

> Therefore, as God's chosen people, holy and dearly loved, clothe yourselves with compassion, kindness, humility, gentleness and patience. Bear with each other and forgive whatever grievances you may have against one another. Forgive as the Lord forgave you. And over all these virtues put on love, which binds them all together in perfect unity.
>
> Let the peace of Christ rule in your hearts, since as members of one body you were called to peace. And be thankful. Let the word of Christ dwell in you richly as you teach

and admonish one another with all wisdom, and as you sing psalms, hymns and spiritual songs with gratitude in your hearts to God. (3:12–16)

In his famous discourse in 1 Corinthians, Paul describes for us the life of a person who is captivated by love. This is a helpful description of life in Christ: "God is love. Whoever lives in love lives in God, and God in him" (1 John 4:16).

> Love is patient, love is kind. It does not envy, it does not boast, it is not proud. It is not rude, it is not self-seeking, it is not easily angered, it keeps no record of wrongs. Love does not delight in evil but rejoices with the truth. It always protects, always trusts, always hopes, always perseveres.
>
> Love never fails. (1 Corinthians 13:4–8a)

Paul isn't the only apostle to instruct us in the fruits of the Spirit. Peter does as well when he writes, "For this very reason, make every effort to add to your faith goodness; and to goodness, knowledge; and to knowledge, self-control; and to self-control, perseverance; and to perseverance, godliness; and to godliness, brotherly kindness; and to brotherly kindness, love" (2 Peter 1:5–7).

Every virtue listed here, every character trait engendered by the Spirit, could fill a whole meditation session: Goodness. Knowledge. Tenderhearted pity. Mercy. The life lived in these virtues would be a beautiful one indeed.

The Fruits are About Character

Nowhere in Scripture do we find an exhaustive list of the fruits of the Spirit. What we do find is the repeated assertion that accepting Christ into your life has consequences for your character. You won't be given a magic touch or supernatural abilities (though the Spirit does shower his gifts where he wills). You won't be transformed into a political activist (though you will undoubtedly become a more just person, which may lead you to take an active role in your community). You won't be given permission to tell people what to do with their lives and butt in where you're not wanted (though you may receive supernatural insights and a word of knowledge from time to time). No, these are not the fruits of the Spirit.

The fruits of the Spirit are about character, and they mark you out as a follower of Christ. Over and over again, Jesus says that people will know his disciples by the fruit they bear. His disciples will be good, holy people. "Each tree is recognized by its own fruit," he tell us. "People do not pick figs from thornbushes, or grapes from briers" (Luke 6:44).

Through regular meditation on God's Word, the Spirit will develop within you a character like Christ's. He will lead you into compassion and humility, away from gossip and backbiting; he will lead you toward chastity, away from lust and loose morals; he will take away your empty speech and quick temper, and replace it with wisdom and patience.

When we move into a house or an apartment, that place begins to take on our characteristics. We fashion it into the sort of place we want to live. Just like that, when the Spirit makes his home within us, we take on his characteristics. He fashions us into a place where he wants to live. Just like we paint the walls our favorite color and hang the pictures we like to look at, the Spirit adorns our soul with love, joy, and peace. Gentleness and charity are his favorite colors. The picture he likes best of all is a joyful, Christlike soul.

It Takes a While to Grow Fruit

It is important to understand that none of this is automatic. You don't water a tree twice and find ripe fruit on it the next day. Growing fruit is a slow, laborious exercise. So you'll need to pray and meditate regularly if you want the Spirit to bear fruit in your soul. I say regularly; not once a month. You could sit down to meditate on God's Word every day and it wouldn't be too much.

That's not to say the Lord can't give you fruit whenever and however he likes. He can raise a plant in one night; just ask Jonah (Jonah 4:6). He can make an abusive man gentle in one afternoon; just ask Paul (Acts 9:3). We don't control God through meditation; he'll grow fruit *when* and *how* he wants to. But we can say that his normal pattern seems to be the same as with the trees: he takes his time.

We Don't Control the Spirit

Don't take from this discussion on the fruits of the Spirit that we do everything for ourselves. We aren't saving ourselves through meditation. It isn't a work of righteousness, where we somehow control the Spirit and make him produce goodness within us. Meditation is nothing more or less than sitting still long enough to listen to the voice of God speaking in you. Don't make the mistake of thinking, as some have, that we can make ourselves perfect through meditation.

We can't be good without the Spirit of God producing goodness within us. But if we do want to be good, then we've got to open the doors to the Spirit and let him in to do some serious redecorating. All Christlikeness—all real beauty of character—is the work of the Spirit. He bears the fruit, not us. We are not naturally virtuous. In fact, Paul contrasts the fruits of the Spirit with the fruits of our sinful nature when he says:

> The acts of the sinful nature are obvious: sexual immorality, impurity and debauchery; idolatry and witchcraft; hatred, discord, jealousy, fits of rage, selfish ambition, dissensions, factions and envy; drunkenness, orgies, and the like. I warn you, as I did before, that those who live like this will not inherit the kingdom of God. (Galatians 5:19–21)

But Christ has not left us in our sins. When a soul reaches out to him, he sends the Spirit to live there. Opening yourself up to the Spirit through meditation is like opening the windows in a room to let the breeze in. The breeze drives out the stench and brings in the scent of sunshine and flowers. And the more often you open the windows, the more pleasant the room will be. But it is the breeze that clears the air, not the person who opens the window.

It is important to remember that, by the Spirit of God, meditation can bring about tremendous change in our lives: it can bring physical health to our bodies, psychological health to our souls, relational health, as well as spiritual benefits yet to be revealed.[13]

---

13. Information in this chapter derived primarily from this book: Boshart Jr., David Holt. "Gifts of the Holy Spirit." Christian Bible Teaching Ministry and Shopping Mall Megasite - Christ-Centered Mall. 1998. Web. 07 Dec. 2011. <http://www.christcenteredmall.com>.

Chapter 15

Falling Deeper in Love with Jesus Christ

The Gifts of the Holy Spirit

Meditating on the Word of God carries with it many benefits, but they all come together in the gifts conferred on the believer by the Holy Spirit. What are the gifts of the Holy Spirit? Actually, there are so many of them it seems kind of silly to try and list them all. Nevertheless, we can speak intelligently about them because Paul lists several when writing to the Corinthians.

> Now to each one the manifestation of the Spirit is given for the common good. To one there is given through the Spirit the message of wisdom, to another the message of knowledge by means of the same Spirit, to another faith by the same Spirit, to another gifts of healing by that one Spirit, to another miraculous powers, to another prophecy, to another distinguishing between spirits, to another speaking in different kinds of tongues, and to still another the interpretation of tongues. All these are the work of one and the same Spirit, and he gives them to each one, just as he determines. (1 Corinthians 12:7–11)

In this one passage Paul lists nine gifts of the Holy Spirit:

- The message of wisdom
- The message of knowledge
- The gift of faith
- The gift of healing
- The working of miracles
- The gift of prophecy
- The discerning of spirits
- Speaking in different kinds of tongues
- The interpretation of tongues

I'll say a little about each one below (though I'm going to reverse the first two, for reasons that will be obvious soon).

The Word of Knowledge

The Creator is omniscient; he knows all things wholly and perfectly. We, on the other hand, are human; we know things partially and imperfectly. There are times in the believer's life, however, when the Holy Spirit transmits to us knowledge we could not otherwise have. That's a supernatural insight into the facts, but we didn't parcel it out ourselves. We received it from God. The message of knowledge comes to us in a variety of ways, from insight into how to solve a particular problem to knowledge of a loved one in danger. There is literally nothing the Holy Spirit can't reveal to the believer, if he so chooses.

The message of knowledge can come at any time. You might be asleep; you might be at work or at home or at church. Generally, when God sends a word, you should act on it. Sometimes you will receive a word of knowledge while you're meditating. It's hard to know what to say about that. Our impulse is always to stop meditating and go act on that word, or communicate it if it bears repeating. Be careful, though—that word might not come from God at all. It might come from the deceiver, trying to throw you off, trying to keep you from prayer. The devil is a liar, and he likes nothing better than to distract you from communion with Jesus. If he senses you getting closer to the Lord in meditation, he'll try to distract you with noises and phone calls and hunger pains. And if he can't distract you with those, he might try to distract you with a sense of urgency about a word he planted there.

The believer must use his or her own head in those situations and have a firm reliance on the Lord. He must test the spirits. But that's true whether the word comes to you in meditation or in the vegetable aisle at the grocery store. Just be aware that, while the message of knowledge is a gift of the Holy Spirit, the sense of urgency to get up and leave off praying can be used by the devil. Ask the Spirit to enlighten you about what to do in those cases, and he will. It could be helpful to have a pen and paper handy, writing down those words that come to mind so you can act on them after your done communing with the Lord.

The Word of Wisdom

Many people confuse wisdom with knowledge. They are related, but where knowledge refers to the comprehension of facts, wisdom refers to the comprehension of value. Where knowledge comes from education, wisdom comes from life experience. You may have noticed that there are many people in your life who are knowledgeable about this-or-that, but few people in your life who are truly wise.

We all rely on wisdom to get us through problems; we draw on our store of wisdom to navigate troubled waters. Sometimes, though, a believer needs supernatural wisdom — wisdom that goes beyond his or her specific experience. Suddenly, he or she understands the value and worth of a person or plan in a way he simply can't account for. That's the Holy Spirit speaking a word of wisdom "from above," where all true worth and value is known.

Jesus is the Wisdom of God. When we commune with Jesus in meditation, we are communing with God's Wisdom, and we gain messages of wisdom that aren't bound by our single solitary experiences.

The Gift of Faith

The gift of faith is the supernatural ability to believe God without doubt, combat unbelief, and visualize what God wants to accomplish. It is not only an inner conviction impelled by an urgent and higher calling, but also a supernatural ability to meet adverse circumstances with trust in God's words and messages.

The Bible speaks of several different types of faith which increase from faith to faith (Romans 1:17):

- Saving faith — faith which gets you into heaven (Ephesians 2:8–9).
- Fruit of faith — faith which gets heaven into you (Galatians 5:22–23).
- Gift of faith — stems from saving faith and the fruit of faith. It is the ability to believe for the miraculous (2 Thessalonians 1:3).

This gift not only operates in healings and in miracles, but in the realm of the impossible as well. Saving faith produces the active faith of the fruit of the Spirit which, in turn, produces the gift of faith. When the gift of faith is employed, the results are miraculous!

We all possess a measure of faith already, given to us by the Lord himself. But many times circumstances require us to step out in faith in a way, and to a degree, we would never have thought possible. We are scared. Maybe we even despair. In those times the Holy Spirit adds to our faith from his ample store. God leads us out of our *comfort zone,* and we find that he's there to catch us, just as he was all along.

Christ is the faithfulness of God. When we spend time with him in meditation and prayer, we receive a double portion of faith—enough to get us through whatever hard times lie ahead.

The Gifts of Healing

The gifts of healing refers to supernatural healing without human aid; it is a special gift to pray for specific diseases. Healing can come through the touch of faith (James 5:14–15); by speaking the word of faith (Luke 7:1–10); or by the presence of God being manifested (Mark 6:56; Acts 19:11–12). The Bible speaks of gifts of healing because there are three types of healings: physical (diabetes, blindness, cancer, deafness, etc.), spiritual (bitterness, greed, and guilt, etc.) and emotional (jealousy, anger etc.).

Although there are three main types of healings, there is much diversity within the gift of healings. While one person might have the gift of healing to rid a person of cancer or perform a creative miracle, another person might have a diversity of the same gift to correct lower back problems or remove a root of bitterness.

According to Mark 16:17–20, the gifts of healing belong to *all* believers. You can know whether or not you have the gift of healing by the following:

- By the inner witness of the Holy Spirit (Romans 8:16).
- When you have a special ability to believe for physical healing for someone (Romans 12:3–8).
- When you have an overwhelming feeling of compassion which moves you to action (Matthew 20:34).

Jesus healed people and he wants us to heal people too. He's given power to his church to heal in his name. I've seen people healed of all sorts of infirmities by the grace of God. Those who have been around Jesus for a while know he loves to work miracles.

Of course, the gifts of healing don't always translate into the sort of instantaneous leave-your-crutches-behind sort of healing we see in church and on television. The gift is paired to the person. For many people, the gift of healing is manifested in greater empathy and compassion, and a willingness to bear one another's burdens. That's a quieter version of the same gift, but it's just as real. Sometimes it's not a person's body that needs healing; it's a person's mind and soul.

By regularly opening ourselves up to God in meditation, we put our hearts and bodies at his service, so that he can continue the healing ministry his Son began two thousand years ago.

The Working of Miracles

A miracle is the performance of something which is against the laws of nature; it is a supernatural power to intervene and counteract earthly and evil forces. The word "miracles" comes from the Greek word *dunamis*, meaning "power and might that multiplies itself." The gift of miracles operates closely with the power gifts of faith and healing to bring authority over Satan, sickness, sin, and the binding forces of these times.

The Bible is full of miracles. But miracles aren't something that happened "way back when"—they happen now, every day. Nothing is impossible with God, and sometimes the Holy Spirit suffuses the life of a believer to the point where he manifests signs and wonders. Those signs and wonders are meant for the glorification of God, not of the individual performing them. A better appreciation for Jesus' miracles through regular meditation on the gospels helps us understand how God continues to work miracles in our own day, and opens us up to being an agent of miraculous change for someone else.

The Gift of Prophecy

The gift of prophecy edifies, exhorts, and comforts (1 Corinthians 14:3); it helps us build up or strengthen; and it should lead us to the Word of God. It is the ministry of the Holy Spirit to convict of sin, of righteousness, and of the judgment to come (John 16:8–11).

Prophecy is divinely inspired and anointed utterance; a supernatural proclamation in a known language. It is the manifestation of the Spirit of God—not of intellect (1 Corinthians 12:7), and it may be possessed and operated by all who have the infilling of the Holy Spirit (1 Corinthians 14:31). Intellect, faith, and will are operative in this gift, but its exercise is not intellectually based. It is calling forth words from the Spirit of God. The gift of prophecy operates when there is high worship (1 Samuel 10:5–6), when other prophets are present (1 Samuel 10:9–10), and when hands are laid on you by ministers (Acts 19:1–6).

If the Holy Spirit gives you a word of prophecy, don't shrink from it: pay attention and deliver it fearlessly. But again—as we saw with the message of knowledge—don't be foolishly led away from prayer right when you receive one. God is never going to send you a gift or a message that pushes you away from him, even for an instant.

The gift of prophecy, when it comes, is always given *for* something. The Holy Spirit doesn't give frivolous messages and he doesn't perform parlor tricks. If the word of prophecy you receive in meditation seems facetious, it might be the deceiver tempting you away from communion. If you receive a prophetic word during your time of meditation, gently acknowledge that you've received it, finish your time of prayer, and then see if it's still there. God's got all the time in the universe; he'll wait for you.

Here are four common misunderstandings about the gift of prophecy:

> *1) The gift of prophecy (1 Corinthians 12) and the office of the prophet (Ephesians 4:11) are not the same thing.*
>
> There is a ministry of the prophet, but not everyone is a prophet. A boy may wear a Chicago Bulls cap, but that does not mean he plays professional basketball for the Chicago Bulls. You may prophesy, but operating in the simple gift of prophecy does not qualify you to stand in the office of a prophet, much like wearing a Bulls hat does not qualify you to play basketball for the Chicago Bulls—you must also be gifted. To stand in the office of a prophet, one must have a consistent manifestation of at least two of the revelation gifts (word of wisdom, word of knowledge, or discerning of spirits) plus prophecy.
>
> *2) Prophecy is not the interpretation of tongues.*
>
> The Bible says that "greater is he that prophesieth than he that speaketh with tongues" (1 Corinthians 14:5, KJV), even though both are inspired utterances. Tongues, of course, is inspired utterance in an unknown tongue. The interpretation of tongues is inspired utterance telling that which was spoken in the unknown tongues. Prophecy, on the other hand, is inspired utterance in a known tongue. The difference between interpretation of tongues and prophecy is that the former is dependent upon tongues, whereas the latter is not.

3) Prophecy is not prediction only.

Prophecy encompasses both foretelling and forth telling. Foretelling is predicting what will happen in the future, while forth telling is delivering a message from God directly to the person or persons for whom the message was sent. Prophecy is a ministry to make people better and more useful Christians in the present and the future. "He that prophesieth speaketh unto men to edification, and exhortation, and comfort (1 Corinthians 14:3, KJV).

4) Prophecy is not the same thing as preaching.

The words "preach" and "prophesy" come from two entirely different Greek words. To "preach" means to proclaim, announce, cry, or tell. Jesus said, "Go ye into all the world, and preach the gospel to every creature" (Mark 16:15, KJV). Note that he didn't say to prophesy the gospel; he said to "preach the gospel." Prophecy means to "bubble up, to flow forth, or to cause to drop like rain." Teaching and preaching are preplanned, but prophecy is not.

The Discerning of Spirits

Discerning of spirits is the supernatural ability given by the Holy Spirit to perceive the source of a spiritual manifestation and determine whether it is of God (Acts 10:30–35), of the devil (Acts 16:16–18), of man (Acts 8:18–23), or of the world. It is not mind reading, psychic phenomena, or the ability to criticize and find fault in others.

Discerning of spirits must be done by the power of the Holy Spirit; he bears witness with our spirit when something is or is not of God. It is the supernatural power to detect the realm of the spirits and their activities. It employs the power of spiritual insight and exposes the supernatural revelation of plans and purposes of the enemy and his forces. It is a gift which protects and guards your spiritual life.

By opening yourself up to the Spirit, God is going to fill you with a spirit of discernment. This will come from his store of knowledge and wisdom, poured into you through frequent meditation on his Word.

Speaking in Different Kinds of Tongues

Supernatural utterance through the power of the Holy Spirit in a person manifests as spiritual language. The Holy Spirit empowers the tongue to edify believers through both language and music. Diverse tongues is the most misunderstood and dynamic gift in the body of Christ. It is not your prayer language, but it can surface through intercession, a conference, or through the individual.

Speaking in tongues is in languages not known to the speaker; these languages may be existent in the world, revived from some past culture, or unknown in the sense that they are a means of communication inspired by the Holy Spirit (Isaiah 28:11; Mark 16:17; Acts 2:4; 10:44–48; 19:1–7; 1 Corinthians 12:10; 13:1–3; 14:2, 4–22, 26–32).

It is a gift given by the Holy Spirit to have the ability to speak in foreign language(s) not previously studied or to respond to experiences of the Holy Spirit by uttering sounds which those without the gift of interpretation could not understand. At Pentecost the church received the gift to communicate the gospel in foreign languages (Acts 2). God gave his Spirit to all his people to empower them to witness and prophesy. In Corinth some members of the church uttered sounds the rest of the congregation did not understand (1 Corinthians 12–14). This led to controversy and division. Paul tried to unite the church, assuring them that there are different gifts but only one Spirit (1 Corinthians 12:4–11).

The Bible speaks of three different types of tongues:

> 1) An unknown tongue unto God (1 Corinthians 14:2). This type of tongue edifies you (1 Corinthians 14:4; Jude 20), assists you in prayer (Romans 8:26–27), stirs up the prophetic ministry (1 Corinthians 14:5), refreshes your soul (Isaiah 28:11–12), gives victory over the devil (Ephesians 6:18), and helps you worship in the Spirit (1 Corinthians 14:14–15; Hebrews 2:12). When you sing in the Spirit, God joins in with you and confuses and defeats the enemy (Isaiah 30:29–31), breaking the yoke of bondage (Acts 16:25), bringing you into the presence of God (Psalm 22:3), and aiding you in intercession (Romans 8:26).
>
> 2) A known tongue that is a sign to unbelievers (1 Corinthians 14:2; Acts 2:6).
>
> 3) A tongue that is understood through interpretation, thus edifying the church (1 Corinthians 14:15).

Remember that the gift of tongues and your prayer language are a product of you and God. The Spirit gives the utterance but you must do the talking.

The Interpretation of Tongues

The interpretation of tongues is a supernatural verbalization and subsequent interpretation to reveal the meaning of a diverse tongue. This gift operates out of the mind of the Spirit rather than out of the mind of man. It is important to note that "interpretation" of tongues is not the same thing as "translation" of tongues, for the interpreter never understands the tongue he or she is interpreting.

The message in tongues may be long and the interpretation short because the interpretation only gives the meaning. On the other hand, one may speak a short time in tongues and then given a very lengthy interpretation. Yet still, at other times, the interpretation is almost word for word.

The Word of God says that if you pray in tongues, you should pray that you will also interpret, not only for the benefit of others but for your own benefit as well.

If someone speaks in tongues, you can ask God to move through you to give the interpretation so others will understand and be edified, but you can also do this in your private time of meditation and prayer for your own personal benefit. You can pray, "Father, in the name of Jesus, give the understanding of what I've just said to you in the Spirit," and the Lord will give you the interpretation.

Gifts for the Church

All nine of these gifts of the Holy Spirit—and the hundreds of others we experience every day—are meant for the glorification of God and the good of the church. While it might seem otherwise, these are gifts that are meant to be shared, not hoarded, and certainly not to be puffed up about.

Meditating on God's Word opens us up to the movement of the Spirit. He's not stingy; he wants to share his gifts with us. And he wants us to share his gifts with others.

Deeper Love of God: A More Intimate Relationship with Him

It's been said that prayer is our talking to God and meditation is God talking to us. I like that because it emphasizes that both prayer and meditation are about relationship. If we don't pray, it's difficult to see how we have a relationship with God; but without some quiet time for reflection and communion, it's hard to see how that relationship is going to deepen.

Do you agree with that last statement: that meditation is all-but-necessary if we're going to enjoy intimacy with God? If not, let's cast this in terms of a marriage: if you're married and all you do is talk at your spouse—you don't stop to listen, you make no time to be with them, your "conversations" are just one long list of complaints about your kids, your job, your paycheck, your car, your house—then that relationship is going to be pretty lopsided. It won't be very intimate because intimacy in a marriage—or any relationship really—involves give-and-take, speaking and listening, periods of quiet "alone time" when you do nothing but sit in each other's presence. The mark of a deep relationship is not how much you have to talk about; it's how long you're willing to sit together in silence once you've run out of things to say.

In marriage, we call those times "comfortable silences." And they are comfortable; you have moved to a deeper, more intimate relationship with each other. You would talk if there was something that needed to be said, but the relationship no longer depends on keeping the conversation going.

Likewise, a regular period of meditation on the Word of God is going to deepen your love for God because it's a comfortable silence. God will say something if there's something that needs to be said; so will you, for that matter. But the relationship no longer depends on it. Sometimes you speak and he listens; sometimes he speaks and you listen; and sometimes you just sit comfortably with each other.

Now, of course, we have to keep in mind that the other basis of intimacy is honesty. If we're not perfectly honest with someone, then we can't be truly intimate with them. True intimacy is founded on perfect honesty. So it is with God: don't expect great periods of quiet intimacy with God when you have sins of which you need to repent. You need to spend some time searching your heart before you start meditating on the Word, confessing to God the things you've said, done, and thought that deliberately flouted his will. You know what they are, and so does he. There's no use beating around the bush with God. Confess your faults and ask forgiveness before you sit down with your

Bible, because meditation without an acknowledgement of your own sinfulness doesn't further intimacy with God at all. Quite the opposite in fact: it drives a wedge between you and the Father.

Jesus tells us in John's gospel, "Remain in me...Remain in my love" (15:7,9). The love of God is his presence. Contrary to everything you've seen on television or at the movies, love is not a feeling. It's true that love often manifests itself in feelings at first; but in the end, love is an act. Love is an act of commitment, manifested in the things we do, the way we live, and the determination not to leave even after the good feelings are gone. People who don't learn this truth say that they're looking for love, but what they're really looking for is infatuation. They find some fascinating person, they feel good, they call it love, and then—when the feelings dampen—they say they're out of love and they move on.

That's not love.

When Jesus tells us to abide in his love, what he means is that we are to manifest our commitment to him even after the good feelings have dampened. Even after we've ceased feeling God's presence in meditation—which, believe me, happens to everyone sooner or later—we still act on our commitment to the relationship. We still grab our Bibles and settle in. Because, just like in a marriage, you don't always have to feel giddy about your spouse to know that you're in love with them.

The real work of intimacy with God is going to happen after you no longer feel much of anything. You'll be tempted to stop. You'll tell me, "Well, I tried meditation for a few months, Pastor, but I just don't get anything out of it anymore."

Yes, but Jesus says, "Remain in me...Remain in my love."

Remain. Live there. Live into the commitment. Understand that it's acting out of the commitment, not out of the emotions, that ushers in true intimacy with God.

Deeper Willingness to Act: More Access to the Power of God to Act

Not only does meditation deepen our willingness to act on God's behalf, it gives us access to God's unlimited power. Paul, in Ephesians 3:20, says that God is able to do immeasurably more than all that we can ask or imagine, according to the power that works in us. A born-again believer walks with the power of God inside him, but that power doesn't work automatically. It must be activated with faith.

When we meditate on the Scriptures, knowing them to be the true revelation of the Word of God, then we access the power of God to act. We come to understand God's will for our lives. We act and speak in the strength of the Holy Spirit.

Regular time spent meditating on the Word of God is going to make it real to you, and it's going to give you a word to say to others. In fact, it's going to make you a word for others—a living, breathing manifestation of God's presence for your family, your community, for the whole earth. As you meditate, you'll find more and more of your life is given over to the glory and dominion of God. Your soul will be like a clean mirror, reflecting the light of Christ to others.

God has the ability to produce results in you. Do you believe that? It's not enough to say you believe it; you've got to live it! In living the life of faith, and spending time meditating on his Word, you allow the Holy Spirit to light upon you in the same way he lit upon Jesus at the Jordan River. You allow him to anoint you—you allow him to "Christ" you. Christ, after all, means "the anointed one." The Father wants us to understand that he will send the Holy Spirit upon us, just as he did for the Son, and make us all into "little Christs," "little anointed ones."

When the enemy sees you and hears you, he's going to stand at attention—not because of you, but because of the anointing and glory smeared on your voice, smeared on your countenance, smeared on everything you do. He will stand back because God is on you, the Word is in you, and the Word is operating through you. You will speak the Word—you will speak God! And when you speak God, hell has got to back up.

Meditation is going to give you a deeper willingness to act, and it's also going to allow God to do exceedingly more through you than you could ever ask or imagine.

Appendix A
Words to Use as a Mantra

Names of Jesus

Jesus	Prince of Peace
Christ	Emmanuel
Messiah	Savior
Anointed One	Good Shepherd
Word of God	The Beloved
Lord	I AM
God	Rabbi
Redeemer	The Alpha and the Omega
King	The Way, the Truth, and the Life
King of Kings	The Resurrection and the Life
Lord of Lords	The Wisdom of God
Son of God	The Man Approved by God
Son of the Father	Wonderful
Son of the Most High	Counselor
Son of Man	Mighty God
Son of David	Everlasting Father
Son of Abraham	Apostle
Son of Mary	High Priest
First Born	Prophet

Servant	Stone of Stumbling
Carpenter	Offering
Nazarene	Sacrifice
Stranger	Mediator
Man of Sorrows	Intercessor
Lamb of God	Advocate
Lamb that was Slain	Gift of God
Lamb without Blemish	Salvation of God
Bridegroom	Redeemer
Light of the City of God	Peace Maker
Temple of the City of God	Consolation of Israel
Door of the Sheep	Just One
Shepherd of Souls	Holy One of Israel
Bishop of Souls	Holy One of God
Chief Shepherd	Firstborn of the Dead
Root of Jesse	Head of the Church
Root of David	Captain of Salvation
Vine	Author and Finisher of Our Faith
Bread of God	Deliverer
True Bread from Heaven	Lion of the Tribe of Judah
Bread of Life	Governor
Rose of Sharon	Lord of the Sabbath
Lily of the Valley	Lord of Peace
Morning Star	Lord of All
Day Star	Glory of Israel
Sun of Righteousness	Righteous Judge
Refuge from the Storm	King of the Jews
Strength to the Needy	King of Saints
Builder	King of the Nations
Foundation	King over all the Earth
Stone	King of Peace
Living Stone	King of Glory
Cornerstone	

Names for God the Father

Abba/Daddy (Romans 8:15)
God Almighty (Genesis 17:1)
Almighty (Revelation 1:8)
Consuming Fire (Deut.eronomy 4:24; Hebrews 12:29)
Creator (Isaiah 43:15; Romans 1:25)
Deliverer (Psalm 18:2)
Eternal God (Deuteronomy 33:27)
Eternal, Immortal, Invisible King (1 Timothy 1:17)
Everlasting Father (Isaiah 9:6)
Father (Matthew 8:9)
Father of Glory (Ephesians 1:17)
Father of Lights (James 1:17)
Father of Mercies (2 Corinthians 1:3)
Father of our Lord Jesus Christ (Colossians 1:3)
Father of Spirits (Hebrews 12:9)
Fortress (Psalm 91:2)
God of Abraham, Isaac, and Jacob (Acts 7:32)
God of All Comfort (2 Corinthians 1:3)
God of Glory (Acts 7:2)
God of Gods (Deuteronomy 10:17)
God of Israel (Matthew 15:31)
God of our Fathers (Acts 7:32)
God of Peace (Hebrews 13:20)
God the Father (2 Timothy 1:2)
Heaven (Matthew 21:25)
Holy One of Israel (Psalm 71:22)
I AM (Exodus 3:14)
Just One (Isaiah 26:7)
King of Israel (2 Samuel 24:23)
King of the Nations (Revelation 15:3)
Lawgiver and Judge (James 4:12)
Light of Israel (Isaiah 10:17)
Light of the Nations (Isaiah 42:6)
Spirit of the Living God (2 Cor. 3:3)
Living God (Joshua 3:10)
Lord Almighty (2 Corinthians 6:18)
Lord God (Acts 3:22)
Lord God of Hosts (James 5:4)
Lord God of Israel (Luke 1:68)
Lord of Lords (Deuteronomy 10:17)
Majestic Glory (2 Peter 1:17)
Majesty (Hebrews 1:3)
Mighty One of Jacob (Isaiah 60:16)
Most High (Deuteronomy 32:8)
Most High God (Hebrews 7:1)
Our Strength (Exodus 15:2)
Power (Mark 14:62)
Prince of Peace (Isaiah 9:6)
Refuge (Psalm 90:1)
Rock (Psalm 18:2)
Rock of Israel (2 Samuel 23:3)
Shepherd (Psalm 23:1)
Sovereign (1 Timothy 6:15)
Stronghold (Psalm 18:2)
Wonderful Counselor (Isaiah 9:6)

Names for the Holy Spirit

A Dove (Matthew 3:16)
Advocate (John 14:16)
Anointing from the Holy One (1 John 2:20)
Breath of God (Genesis 2:6–7)
Breath of the Almighty (Job 33:4)
Comforter (John 14:26; 16:7)
Defender (Proverbs 23:11)
Eternal Spirit (Hebrews 9:14)
Fire (Acts 2:3)
Free Spirit (Psalm 51:12)
Good Spirit (Nehemiah 9:20)
Holy Spirit of God (Ephesians 4:30)
Like breath (John 20:22)
Like clothing (Luke 24:49)
Like oil (Acts 10:38)
Like wind (John 3:8)
Like wine (Ephesians 5:18)
Love of God (Romans 5:5)
Pledge and down payment of our inheritance (2 Corinthians 1:22)
Power of God (Luke 1:35)
Power of the Highest (Luke 1:35)
Sanctifier (Romans 15:16)
Seal (Ephesians 1:13)
Spirit (Genesis 1:2)
Spirit of Adoption (Romans 8:15)
Spirit of Burning (Isaiah 4:4)
Spirit of Christ (Romans 8:9)
Spirit of Counsel (Isaiah 11:2)
Spirit of Faith (2 Corinthians 4:13)
Spirit of Glory (1 Peter 4:14)
Spirit of God (Romans 8:9)
Spirit of Grace (Hebrews 10:29)
Spirit of Holiness (Romans 1:4)
Spirit of Jesus (Acts 16:7; Phil.1:19)
Spirit of Judgment (Isaiah 4:4)
Spirit of Knowledge (Isaiah 11:2)
Spirit of Life (Romans 8:2; Rev. 11:11)
Spirit of Love (1 Timothy 1:7)
Spirit of Might (Isaiah 11:2)
Spirit of Promise (Ephesians 1:13)
Spirit of Prophecy (Revelation 19:10)
Spirit of Revelation (Ephesians 1:17)
Spirit of Supplication (Zech.12:10)
Spirit of the Father (Matthew 10:20)
Spirit of the Fear of the Lord (Isaiah 11:2)
Spirit of the Living God (2 Cor. 3:3)
Spirit of the Lord (Luke 4:18; 2 Corinthians 3:17)
Spirit of the Lord God (Isaiah 61:1)
Spirit of the Son (Galatians 4:6)
Spirit of Truth (John 14:17)
Spirit of Understanding (Isaiah 11:2)
Spirit of Wisdom (Ephesians 1:17)
The Holy Spirit (Luke 3:16)
The Holy Spirit of God (Eph. 4:30)
The Holy Spirit of Promise (Eph. 1:13)
The Spirit (Romans 2:29)
Voice of the Almighty (Ezekiel 1:24)
Voice of the Lord (Deuteronomy 4:30)
Water (John 7:38)

Attributes of God

Able to defend us (Psalm 59:9–11)
Able to deliver us (Daniel 3–4)
Able to do all things (Mark 14:36)
Able to do the impossible (Luke 1:34–37)
Able to do what he has promised (Romans 4:21)
Able to forgive sins (Matthew 9:6)
Able to protect us (Psalm 79:1)
Able to raise the dead (Hebrews 11:17–19)
Able to rescue us (Psalm 79:11)
Able to save us (Isaiah 63:1)
All-knowing (Psalm 139:1–6)
All-powerful (Jer. 32:17; Matt.6:13)
All-wise (Romans 11:33)
Always acting for our good (Proverbs 3:19–20)
Angry at the evil men do (Nahum 1:2–8)
Beginning and ending of true prayer (Hebrews 4:14–16)
Benevolent (Psalm 119:65–72)
Comes to our aid in temptation (Hebrews 2:18)
Comforter (2 Corinthians 1:3–4)
Empowers us to spread the Good News (Matthew 28:18–20)
Everywhere present (Psalm 139:7–12)
Faithful (Psalm 89:1–8)
Father (Romans 8:15–17)
Giver of spiritual gifts (Ephesians 3:7)
Giver of victory (1 Corinthians 15:57)
God alone is wise (Romans 16:25–27)
Gracious and forgiving (Eph.1:5–8)
Great in goodness (Psalm 31:19)
Head of the church (Eph. 1:22–23)
Healing (Exodus 15:22–26)
Holy and apart (Revelation 4:8–11)
In control of our lives (1 Chr.onicles 29:11–13)
Infinite (Romans 11:33)
Just (Psalm 75:1–7)
Keeps us from falling (Jude 1:24–25)
Kind to men (Psalm 107:1)
Lord (2 Samuel 7:18–20)
Loving (1 John 4:7–10)
Merciful and compassionate (Deuteronomy 4:29–31)
Mighty and strong (Genesis 17:7–8)
Peace-giving (Judges 6:16–24)
Possessing all authority (Ex. 3:13–15)
Providing (Genesis 22:9–14)
Sanctifier (Leviticus 20:7–8)
Self-sufficient (Acts 17:24–28)
Shows his power in weakness (2 Corinthians 12:9–10)
Source of all blessings (Gen. 49:22–26)
Source of all good (James 1:17)
Source of true wisdom (James 1:5)
Speaks to us simply (1 Corinthians 1)
Transcendent (Psalm 113:4–5)
Unchanging (Psalm 102:25–28)
Wise and mighty (Job 12:13)
Wiser than men (Isaiah 55:8–9)
Withholds nothing good from his children (Psalm 84:11)

Appendix B
Phrases to Use as a Mantra

- My Lord and my God.
- Lord, I believe. Help my unbelief.
- Let it be done according to your word.
- Jesus Christ, Son of God, have mercy on me, a sinner.
- Glory to God in the highest.
- My soul proclaims the greatness of the Lord.
- Jesus is Lord.
- Come, Holy Spirit.
- Our Father, who art in heaven, hallowed be thy name.
- In the beginning was the Word and the Word was with God and the Word was God.
- What shall separate us from the love of Christ?
- God is love.
- Into your hands, I commend my spirit.
- He is not here, he is risen.
- Go and sin no more.
- I am the Alpha and the Omega.
- Lord, you have now set your servant free to go in peace as you have promised.

- Son of David, have pity on me.
- Thy Word is a lantern to my feet and a light upon my path.
- The Lord is my shepherd, I shall not want.
- Come to me all you who are heavy laden, and I will give you rest.
- Love is patient, love is kind.
- Faith, hope, and love abide; and the greatest of these is love.
- Unbind him and let him go.
- In the beginning God created the heavens and the earth.
- I have waited for thy salvation, Lord.
- The Lord is my strength and my song.
- Though he slay me, yet will I trust in him.
- Blessed are they that put their trust in him.
- How excellent is thy name in all the earth.
- How long wilt thou forget me, O Lord?
- Taste and see that the Lord is good.
- Be still and know that I am God.
- A broken and contrite heart, O Lord, you will not despise.
- The Lord reigns, let the earth rejoice.
- To everything there is a season, and a time to every purpose under heaven.

Appendix C
Bible Verses to Meditate On

For Strength

Isaiah 40:28–31: Do you not know? Have you not heard? The Lord is the everlasting God, the Creator of the ends of the earth. He will not grow tired or weary, and his understanding no one can fathom. He gives strength to the weary and increases the power of the weak. Even youths grow tired and weary, and young men stumble and fall; but those who hope in the Lord will renew their strength. They will soar on wings like eagles; they will run and not grow weary; they will walk and not be faint.

Isaiah 41:10: So do not fear, for I am with you; do not be dismayed, for I am your God. I will strengthen you and help you; I will uphold you with my righteous right hand.

1 Chronicles 16:11: Look to the Lord and his strength; seek his face always.

Exodus 15:2: The Lord is my strength and my defense; he has become my salvation. He is my God, and I will praise him, my father's God, and I will exalt him.

Philippians 4:13: I can do all this through him who gives me strength.

Psalm 18:32–34: It is God who arms me with strength and keeps my way secure. He makes my feet like the feet of a deer; he causes me to stand on the heights. He trains my hands for battle; my arms can bend a bow of bronze.

1 Corinthians 10:13: No temptation has overtaken you except what is common to mankind. And God is faithful; he will not let you be tempted beyond what you can bear. But when you are tempted, he will also provide a way out so that you can endure it.

Psalm 119:23: Though rulers sit together and slander me, your servant will meditate on your decrees.

1 Samuel 30:6: David was greatly distressed because the men were talking of stoning him; each one was bitter in spirit because of his sons and daughters. But David found strength in the Lord his God.

2 Timothy 4:17: But the Lord stood at my side and gave me strength, so that through me the message might be fully proclaimed and all the Gentiles might hear it. And I was delivered from the lion's mouth.

1 Peter 4:11: If anyone speaks, they should do so as one who speaks the very words of God. If anyone serves, they should do so with the strength God provides, so that in all things God may be praised through Jesus Christ.

Joshua 1:9: Have I not commanded you? Be strong and courageous. Do not be afraid; do not be discouraged, for the Lord your God will be with you wherever you go.

Psalm 27:1: The Lord is my light and my salvation — whom shall I fear? The Lord is the stronghold of my life — of whom shall I be afraid?

Matthew 17:20 Jesus replied, "Because you have so little faith. Truly I tell you, if you have faith as small as a mustard seed, you can say to this mountain, 'Move from here to there,' and it will move. Nothing will be impossible for you."

Deuteronomy 31:6: Be strong and courageous. Do not be afraid or terrified because of them, for the Lord your God goes with you; he will never leave you nor forsake you.

Zephaniah 3:17: The Lord your God is with you, the Mighty Warrior who saves. He will take great delight in you; in his love he will no longer rebuke you, but will rejoice over you with singing.

2 Corinthians 4:16–18: Therefore we do not lose heart. Though outwardly we are wasting away, yet inwardly we are being renewed day by day. For our light and momentary troubles are achieving for us an eternal glory that far outweighs them all. So we fix our eyes not on what is seen, but on what is unseen, since what is seen is temporary, but what is unseen is eternal.

2 Timothy 1:7: For the Spirit God gave us does not make us timid, but gives us power, love and self-discipline.

2 Corinthians 12:9: But he said to me, "My grace is sufficient for you, for my power is made perfect in weakness." Therefore I will boast all the more gladly about my weaknesses, so that Christ's power may rest on me.

For Comfort

Numbers 6:24–26: The Lord bless you and keep you; the Lord make his face shine on you and be gracious to you; the Lord turn his face toward you and give you peace.

Joshua 1:9: Have I not commanded you? Be strong and courageous. Do not be afraid; do not be discouraged, for the Lord your God will be with you wherever you go.

Psalm 16:8: I keep my eyes always on the Lord. With him at my right hand, I will not be shaken.

Psalm 23:1, 3–4: The Lord is my shepherd, I lack nothing. He refreshes my soul. He guides me along the right paths for his name's sake. Even though I walk through the darkest valley, I will fear no evil, for you are with me; your rod and your staff, they comfort me.

Psalm 27:1: The Lord is my light and my salvation—whom shall I fear? The Lord is the stronghold of my life—of whom shall I be afraid?

Psalm 34:4: I sought the Lord, and he answered me; he delivered me from all my fears.

Psalm 46:1: God is our refuge and strength, an ever-present help in trouble.

Psalm 91:5–7: You will not fear the terror of night, nor the arrow that flies by day, nor the pestilence that stalks in the darkness, nor the plague that destroys at midday. A thousand may fall at your side, ten thousand at your right hand, but it will not come near you.

Psalm 94:18–19: When I said, "My foot is slipping," your unfailing love, Lord, supported me. When anxiety was great within me, your consolation brought me joy.

Psalm 116:1–2: I love the Lord, for he heard my voice; he heard my cry for mercy. Because he turned his ear to me, I will call on him as long as I live.

Psalm 119:114: You are my refuge and my shield; I have put my hope in your word.

Isaiah 26:4: Trust in the Lord forever, for the Lord, the Lord himself, is the Rock eternal.

Daniel 2:20–22: Praise be to the name of God for ever and ever; wisdom and power are his. He changes times and seasons; he deposes kings and raises up others. He gives wisdom to the wise and knowledge to the discerning. He reveals deep and hidden things; he knows what lies in darkness, and light dwells with him.

Matthew 19:26: Jesus looked at them and said, "With man this is impossible, but with God all things are possible."

John 10:10b: I have come that they may have life, and have it to the full.

John 14:27: Peace I leave with you; my peace I give you. I do not give to you as the world gives. Do not let your hearts be troubled and do not be afraid.

Romans 8:35, 37: Who shall separate us from the love of Christ? Shall trouble or hardship or persecution or famine or nakedness or danger or sword? No, in all these things we are more than conquerors through him who loved us.

Romans 8:38–39: For I am convinced that neither death nor life, neither angels nor demons, neither the present nor the future, nor any powers, neither height nor depth, nor anything else in all creation, will be able to separate us from the love of God that is in Christ Jesus our Lord.

Colossians 3:12–14: Therefore, as God's chosen people, holy and dearly loved, clothe yourselves with compassion, kindness, humility, gentleness and patience. Bear with each other and forgive one another if any of you has a grievance against someone. Forgive as the Lord forgave you. And over all these virtues put on love, which binds them all together in perfect unity.

Hebrews 13:6: So we say with confidence, "The Lord is my helper; I will not be afraid. What can mere mortals do to me?"

For Repentance

Leviticus 26:40, 42: But if they will confess their sins and the sins of their fathers, I will remember my covenant with Jacob.

Deuteronomy 4:29: If from there you seek the Lord your God, you will find him if you look for him with all your heart and with all your soul.

Deuteronomy 4:31: For the Lord your God is a merciful God; he will not abandon or destroy you or forget the covenant with your forefathers.

2 Samuel 24:10: I have sinned greatly in what I have done. Now, O Lord, I beg you, take away the guilt of your servant. I have done a very foolish thing.

2 Chronicles 7:14: If my people, who are called by my name, will humble themselves and pray and seek my face and turn from their wicked ways, then will I hear from heaven and will forgive their sin.

Ezra 9:6: O my God, I am too ashamed and disgraced to lift up my face to you, my God, because our sins are higher than our heads and our guilt has reached to the heavens.

Nehemiah 1:7: We have acted very wickedly toward you. We have not obeyed the commands, decrees and laws you gave your servant Moses.

Nehemiah 9:33: In all that has happened to us, you have been just; you have acted faithfully, while we did wrong.

Job 33:27: Then he comes to men and says, "I sinned, and perverted what was right, but I did not get what I deserved."

Psalm 32:5: Then I acknowledged my sin to you and did not cover up my iniquity. I said, "I will confess my transgressions to the Lord" — and you forgave the guilt of my sin.

Psalm 34:14: Turn from evil and do good; seek peace and pursue it.

Psalm 34:17: The righteous cry out, and the Lord hears them; he delivers them from all their troubles.

Psalm 34:18: The Lord is close to the brokenhearted and saves those who are crushed in spirit.

Psalm 38:17: My guilt has overwhelmed me like a burden too heavy to bear.

Psalm 38:18: I confess my iniquity; I am troubled by my sin.

Psalm 51:1–2, 10: Have mercy on me, O God, according to your unfailing love; according to your great compassion blot out my transgressions. Wash away all my iniquity and cleanse me from my sin....Create in me a pure heart, O God, and renew a steadfast spirit within me.

Psalm 69:5: You know my folly, O God; my guilt is not hidden from you.

Psalm 119:176: I have strayed like a lost sheep. Seek your servant, for I have not forgotten your commands.

Matthew 3:2: Repent, for the kingdom of heaven is near.

Mark 2:17: On hearing this, Jesus said to them, "It is not the healthy who need a doctor, but the sick. I have not come to call the righteous, but sinners."

For Discernment

Philippians 4:8: Finally, brothers, whatever is true, whatever is noble, whatever is right, whatever is pure, whatever is lovely, whatever is admirable--if anything is excellent or praiseworthy--think about such things.

1 John 4:1: Do not believe every spirit, but test the spirits to see whether they are from God, because many false prophets have gone out into the world.

Philippians 1:9–10: This is my prayer: that your love may abound more and more in knowledge and depth of insight, so that you may be able to discern what is best and may be pure and blameless until the day of Christ, filled with the fruit of righteousness that comes through Jesus Christ — to the glory and praise of God.

1 Corinthians 14:33: God is not a God of disorder but of peace.

1 Kings 3:9: Give your servant a discerning heart to distinguish between right and wrong.

2 Corinthians 11:14: Satan himself masquerades as an angel of light.

Matthew 24:24: False Christs and false prophets will appear and perform great signs and miracles to deceive even the elect — if that were possible.

Psalm 34:18: The Lord is close to the brokenhearted and saves those who are crushed in spirit.

Colossians 2:8: See to it that no one takes you captive through hollow and deceptive philosophy, which depends on human tradition and the basic principles of this world rather than on Christ.

Proverbs 2:1–5: My son, if you accept my words and store up my commands within you, turning your ear to wisdom and applying your heart to understanding, and if you call out for insight and cry aloud for understanding, and if you look for it as for silver and search for it as for hidden treasure, then you will understand the fear of the Lord and find the knowledge of God.

For Needs

Psalm 91:14–15: "Because he loves me," says the Lord, "I will rescue him; I will protect him, for he acknowledges my name. He will call upon me, and I will answer him; I will be with him in trouble, I will deliver him and honor him."

Isaiah 41:10: So do not fear, for I am with you; do not be dismayed, for I am your God. I will strengthen you and help you; I will uphold you with my righteous right hand.

Psalm 91:1–2: Whoever dwells in the shelter of the Most High will rest in the shadow of the Almighty. I will say of the Lord, "He is my refuge and my fortress, my God, in whom I trust."

Psalm 37:25: I have been young, and now am old; yet have I not seen the righteous forsaken, nor their children begging bread.

2 Corinthians 9:8: And God is able to make all grace abound toward you; that ye, always having all sufficiency in all things, may abound to every good work:

Philippians 4:19: But my God shall supply all your need according to his riches in glory by Christ Jesus.

Philippians 4:6: Do not be anxious about anything, but in everything, by prayer and petition, with thanksgiving, present your requests to God.

Psalm 34:9–10: Fear the Lord, you his holy people, for those who fear him lack nothing. The lions may grow weak and hungry, but those who seek the Lord lack no good thing.

Psalm 55:16–17: But I call to God, and the Lord will save me. Evening and morning and at noon I utter my complaint and moan, and he hears my voice.

Matthew 7:7–11: Ask and it will be given to you; seek and you will find; knock and the door will be opened to you. For everyone who asks receives; the one who seeks finds; and to the one who knocks, the door will be opened. Which of you, if your son asks for bread, will give him a stone? Or if he asks for a fish, will give him a snake? If you, then, though you are evil, know how to give good gifts to your children, how much more will your Father in heaven give good gifts to those who ask him!

For Gratitude

1 Chronicles 29:12: Wealth and honor come from you; you are the ruler of all things. In your hands are strength and power to exalt and give strength to all.

1 Chronicles 29:14: But who am I, and who are my people, that we should be able to give as generously as this? Everything comes from you, and we have given you only what comes from your hand.

Psalm 18:49: Therefore I will praise you among the nations, O Lord; I will sing praises to your name.

Psalm 30:4: Sing to the Lord, you saints of his; praise his holy name.

Psalm 35:18: I will give you thanks in the great assembly; among throngs of people I will praise you.

Psalm 69:30: I will praise God's name in song and glorify him with thanksgiving.

Psalm 75:1: We give thanks to you, O God, we give thanks, for your Name is near; men tell of your wonderful deeds.

Psalm 92:1–2: It is good to praise the Lord and make music to your name, O Most High. Let us come before him with thanksgiving and extol him with music and song.

Psalm 97:12: Rejoice in the Lord, you who are righteous, and praise his holy name.

Psalm 100:4: Enter his gates with thanksgiving and his courts with praise; give thanks to him and praise his name.

Psalm 105:1: Give thanks to the Lord, call on his name; make known among the nations what he has done.

Psalm 106:1: Praise the Lord. Give thanks to the Lord, for he is good; his love endures forever.

Psalm 107:1: Give thanks to the Lord, for he is good; his love endures forever.

Psalm 116:17: I will sacrifice a thank offering to you and call on the name of the Lord.

Psalm 136:1: Give thanks to the Lord, for he is good. His love endures forever.

Daniel 2:23: I thank and praise you, O God of my fathers: You have given me wisdom and power, you have made known to me what we asked of you, you have made known to us the dream of the king.

Matthew 11:25: I praise you, Father, Lord of heaven and earth, because you have hidden these things from the wise and learned, and revealed them to little children.

John 11:41: Father, I thank you that you have heard me.

Romans 1:8: I thank my God through Jesus Christ for all of you, because your faith is being reported all over the world.

Romans 6:17: Thanks be to God that, though you used to be slaves to sin, you wholeheartedly obeyed the form of teaching to which you were entrusted.

1 Corinthians 1:4: I always thank God for you because of his grace given you in Christ Jesus.

1 Corinthians 15:57: But thanks be to God! He gives us the victory through our Lord Jesus Christ.

2 Corinthians 2:14: Thanks be to God, who always leads us in triumphal procession in Christ and through us spreads everywhere the fragrance of the knowledge of him.

2 Corinthians 8:16: I thank God, who put into the heart of Titus the same concern I have for you.

2 Corinthians 9:11: You will be made rich in every way so that you can be generous on every occasion, and through us your generosity will result in thanksgiving to God.

2 Corinthians 9:15: Thanks be to God for his indescribable gift!

Philippians 4:6: Do not be anxious about anything, but in everything, by prayer and petition, with thanksgiving, present your requests to God.

For Acceptance of God's Will

John 6:40: For this is the will of God, that everyone who sees the Son and believes in him should have eternal life; and I will raise him up at the last day.

Ephesians 1:10–12: For he has made known to us in all wisdom and insight the mystery of his will, according to his purpose which he set forth in Christ as a plan for the fullness of time, to unite all things in him, things in heaven and things on earth. In him, according to the purpose of Him who accomplishes all things according to the counsel of his will, we who first hoped in Christ have been destined and appointed to live for the praise of his glory.

Ephesians 5:17–20: Therefore do not be foolish, but understand what the Lord's will is. Do not get drunk on wine, which leads to debauchery. Instead, be filled with the Spirit. Speak to one another with psalms, hymns and spiritual songs. Sing and make music in your heart to the Lord, always giving thanks to God the Father for everything, in the name of our Lord Jesus Christ.

Psalm 40:8: I desire to do your will, my God; your law is within my heart.

Colossians 1:9: For this reason, since the day we heard about you, we have not stopped praying for you and asking God to fill you with the knowledge of his will through all spiritual wisdom and understanding.

1 John 2:17: The world and its desires pass away, but the man who does the will of God lives forever.

Romans 12:1–2: Therefore, I urge you, brothers, in view of God's mercy, to offer your bodies as living sacrifices, holy and pleasing to God — this is your spiritual act of worship. Do not conform any longer to the pattern of this world, but be transformed by the renewing of your mind. Then you will be able to test and approve what God's will is — his good, pleasing and perfect will.

Jeremiah 29:11: "For I know the plans I have for you," declares the Lord, "plans to prosper you and not to harm you, plans to give you hope and a future."

Psalm 118:8: It is better to trust in the Lord than to put confidence in man.

Proverbs 3:5–6: Trust in the Lord with all your heart and lean not on your own understanding; In all your ways acknowledge Him, and He will make your paths straight.

Proverbs 16:9: A man's heart plans his way, but the Lord directs his steps.

Appendix D
Passages for Visualization

Matthew 1:18–25

[18] This is how the birth of Jesus the Messiah came about: His mother Mary was pledged to be married to Joseph, but before they came together, she was found to be pregnant through the Holy Spirit. [19] Because Joseph her husband was faithful to the law, and yet did not want to expose her to public disgrace, he had in mind to divorce her quietly.

[20] But after he had considered this, an angel of the Lord appeared to him in a dream and said, "Joseph son of David, do not be afraid to take Mary home as your wife, because what is conceived in her is from the Holy Spirit. [21] She will give birth to a son, and you are to give him the name Jesus, because he will save his people from their sins."

[22] All this took place to fulfill what the Lord had said through the prophet: [23] "The virgin will conceive and give birth to a son, and they will call him Immanuel" (which means "God with us").

[24] When Joseph woke up, he did what the angel of the Lord had commanded him and took Mary home as his wife. [25] But he did not consummate their marriage until she gave birth to a son. And he gave him the name Jesus.

Mark 2:1–12

2:1–5: When he re-entered Capernaum some days later, a rumour spread that he was in somebody's house. Such a large crowd collected that while he was giving them his message it was impossible even to get near the doorway. Meanwhile, a group of people arrived to see him, bringing with them a paralytic whom four of them were carrying. And when they found it was impossible to get near him because of the crowd, they removed the tiles from the roof over Jesus' head and let down the paralytic's bed through the opening. And when Jesus saw their faith, he said to the man on the bed, "My son, your sins are forgiven."

2:6–7: But some of the scribes were sitting there silently asking themselves, "Why does this man talk such blasphemy? Who can possibly forgive sins but God?"

2:8–11: Jesus realized instantly what they were thinking, and said to them, "why must you argue like this in your minds? Which do you suppose is easier — to say to a paralyzed man, 'Your sins are forgiven', or 'Get up, pick up your bed and walk'? But to prove to you that the Son of Man has full authority to forgive sins on earth, I say to you," — and here he spoke to the paralytic — "Get up, pick up your bed and go home."

2:12: At once the man sprang to his feet, picked up his bed and walked off in full view of them all. Everyone was amazed, praised God, and said, "We have never seen anything like this before."

Luke 3:22–38

[22] When the time came for the purification rites required by the Law of Moses, Joseph and Mary took him to Jerusalem to present him to the Lord [23] (as it is written in the Law of the Lord, "Every firstborn male is to be consecrated to the Lord"), [24] and to offer a sacrifice in keeping with what is said in the Law of the Lord: "a pair of doves or two young pigeons."

[25] Now there was a man in Jerusalem called Simeon, who was righteous and devout. He was waiting for the consolation of Israel, and the Holy Spirit was on him. [26] It had been revealed to him by the Holy Spirit that he would not die before he had seen the Lord's Messiah. [27] Moved by the Spirit, he went into the temple courts. When the parents brought in the child Jesus to do for him what the custom of the Law required, [28] Simeon took him in his arms and praised God, saying:

²⁹ "Sovereign Lord, as you have promised,
you may now dismiss your servant in peace.
³⁰ For my eyes have seen your salvation,
³¹ which you have prepared in the sight of all nations:
³² a light for revelation to the Gentiles,
and the glory of your people Israel."

³³ The child's father and mother marveled at what was said about him. ³⁴ Then Simeon blessed them and said to Mary, his mother: "This child is destined to cause the falling and rising of many in Israel, and to be a sign that will be spoken against, ³⁵ so that the thoughts of many hearts will be revealed. And a sword will pierce your own soul too."

³⁶ There was also a prophet, Anna, the daughter of Penuel, of the tribe of Asher. She was very old; she had lived with her husband seven years after her marriage, ³⁷ and then was a widow until she was eighty-four. She never left the temple but worshiped night and day, fasting and praying. ³⁸ Coming up to them at that very moment, she gave thanks to God and spoke about the child to all who were looking forward to the redemption of Jerusalem.

³⁹ When Joseph and Mary had done everything required by the Law of the Lord, they returned to Galilee to their own town of Nazareth. ⁴⁰ And the child grew and became strong; he was filled with wisdom, and the grace of God was on him.

John 2:1–12

¹ On the third day a wedding took place at Cana in Galilee. Jesus' mother was there, ² and Jesus and his disciples had also been invited to the wedding. ³ When the wine was gone, Jesus' mother said to him, "They have no more wine."

⁴ "Woman, why do you involve me?" Jesus replied. "My hour has not yet come."

⁵ His mother said to the servants, "Do whatever he tells you."

⁶ Nearby stood six stone water jars, the kind used by the Jews for ceremonial washing, each holding from twenty to thirty gallons.

⁷ Jesus said to the servants, "Fill the jars with water"; so they filled them to the brim.

⁸ Then he told them, "Now draw some out and take it to the master of the banquet."

They did so, ⁹ and the master of the banquet tasted the water that had been turned into wine. He did not realize where it had come from, though the servants who had drawn the water knew. Then he called the bridegroom aside ¹⁰ and said, "Everyone brings out the choice wine first and then the cheaper wine after the guests have had too much to drink; but you have saved the best till now."

¹¹ What Jesus did here in Cana of Galilee was the first of the signs through which he revealed his glory; and his disciples believed in him.

¹² After this he went down to Capernaum with his mother and brothers and his disciples. There they stayed for a few days.

Acts 2:1–12

¹ When the day of Pentecost came, they were all together in one place. ² Suddenly a sound like the blowing of a violent wind came from heaven and filled the whole house where they were sitting. ³ They saw what seemed to be tongues of fire that separated and came to rest on each of them. ⁴ All of them were filled with the Holy Spirit and began to speak in other tongues as the Spirit enabled them.

⁵ Now there were staying in Jerusalem God-fearing Jews from every nation under heaven. ⁶ When they heard this sound, a crowd came together in bewilderment, because each one heard their own language being spoken. ⁷ Utterly amazed, they asked: "Aren't all these who are speaking Galileans? ⁸ Then how is it that each of us hears them in our native language? ⁹ Parthians, Medes and Elamites; residents of Mesopotamia, Judea and Cappadocia, Pontus and Asia, ¹⁰ Phrygia and Pamphylia, Egypt and the parts of Libya near Cyrene; visitors from Rome ¹¹ (both Jews and converts to Judaism); Cretans and Arabs — we hear them declaring the wonders of God in our own tongues!" ¹² Amazed and perplexed, they asked one another, "What does this mean?"

Matthew 8:5–13

⁵ When Jesus had entered Capernaum, a centurion came to him, asking for help. ⁶ "Lord," he said, "my servant lies at home paralyzed, suffering terribly."

⁷ Jesus said to him, "Shall I come and heal him?"

⁸ The centurion replied, "Lord, I do not deserve to have you come under my roof. But just say the word, and my servant will be healed. ⁹ For I myself am a man under authority, with soldiers under me. I tell this one, 'Go,' and

he goes; and that one, 'Come,' and he comes. I say to my servant, 'Do this,' and he does it."

[10] When Jesus heard this, he was amazed and said to those following him, "Truly I tell you, I have not found anyone in Israel with such great faith. [11] I say to you that many will come from the east and the west, and will take their places at the feast with Abraham, Isaac and Jacob in the kingdom of heaven. [12] But the subjects of the kingdom will be thrown outside, into the darkness, where there will be weeping and gnashing of teeth."

[13] Then Jesus said to the centurion, "Go! Let it be done just as you believed it would." And his servant was healed at that moment.

Mark 5:21–43

[21] When Jesus had again crossed over by boat to the other side of the lake, a large crowd gathered around him while he was by the lake. [22] Then one of the synagogue leaders, named Jairus, came, and when he saw Jesus, he fell at his feet. [23] He pleaded earnestly with him, "My little daughter is dying. Please come and put your hands on her so that she will be healed and live." [24] So Jesus went with him.

A large crowd followed and pressed around him. [25] And a woman was there who had been subject to bleeding for twelve years. [26] She had suffered a great deal under the care of many doctors and had spent all she had, yet instead of getting better she grew worse. [27] When she heard about Jesus, she came up behind him in the crowd and touched his cloak, [28] because she thought, "If I just touch his clothes, I will be healed." [29] Immediately her bleeding stopped and she felt in her body that she was freed from her suffering.

[30] At once Jesus realized that power had gone out from him. He turned around in the crowd and asked, "Who touched my clothes?"

[31] "You see the people crowding against you," his disciples answered, "and yet you can ask, 'Who touched me?' "

[32] But Jesus kept looking around to see who had done it. [33] Then the woman, knowing what had happened to her, came and fell at his feet and, trembling with fear, told him the whole truth. [34] He said to her, "Daughter, your faith has healed you. Go in peace and be freed from your suffering."

[35] While Jesus was still speaking, some people came from the house of Jairus, the synagogue leader. "Your daughter is dead," they said. "Why bother the teacher anymore?"

⁣³⁶ Overhearing what they said, Jesus told him, "Don't be afraid; just believe."

³⁷ He did not let anyone follow him except Peter, James and John the brother of James. ³⁸ When they came to the home of the synagogue leader, Jesus saw a commotion, with people crying and wailing loudly. ³⁹ He went in and said to them, "Why all this commotion and wailing? The child is not dead but asleep." ⁴⁰ But they laughed at him.

After he put them all out, he took the child's father and mother and the disciples who were with him, and went in where the child was. ⁴¹ He took her by the hand and said to her, "Talitha koum!" (which means "Little girl, I say to you, get up!"). ⁴² Immediately the girl stood up and began to walk around (she was twelve years old). At this they were completely astonished. ⁴³ He gave strict orders not to let anyone know about this, and told them to give her something to eat.

Luke 24:1–12

¹ On the first day of the week, very early in the morning, the women took the spices they had prepared and went to the tomb. ² They found the stone rolled away from the tomb, ³ but when they entered, they did not find the body of the Lord Jesus. ⁴ While they were wondering about this, suddenly two men in clothes that gleamed like lightning stood beside them. ⁵ In their fright the women bowed down with their faces to the ground, but the men said to them, "Why do you look for the living among the dead? ⁶ He is not here; he has risen! Remember how he told you, while he was still with you in Galilee: ⁷ 'The Son of Man must be delivered over to the hands of sinners, be crucified and on the third day be raised again.' " ⁸ Then they remembered his words.

⁹ When they came back from the tomb, they told all these things to the Eleven and to all the others. ¹⁰ It was Mary Magdalene, Joanna, Mary the mother of James, and the others with them who told this to the apostles. ¹¹ But they did not believe the women, because their words seemed to them like nonsense. ¹² Peter, however, got up and ran to the tomb. Bending over, he saw the strips of linen lying by themselves, and he went away, wondering to himself what had happened.

John 11:17–44

¹⁷ On his arrival, Jesus found that Lazarus had already been in the tomb for four days. ¹⁸ Now Bethany was less than two miles from Jerusalem, ¹⁹ and many Jews had come to Martha and Mary to comfort them in the loss of their

brother. ²⁰ When Martha heard that Jesus was coming, she went out to meet him, but Mary stayed at home.

²¹ "Lord," Martha said to Jesus, "if you had been here, my brother would not have died. ²² But I know that even now God will give you whatever you ask."

²³ Jesus said to her, "Your brother will rise again."

²⁴ Martha answered, "I know he will rise again in the resurrection at the last day."

²⁵ Jesus said to her, "I am the resurrection and the life. The one who believes in me will live, even though they die; ²⁶ and whoever lives by believing in me will never die. Do you believe this?"

²⁷ "Yes, Lord," she replied, "I believe that you are the Messiah, the Son of God, who is to come into the world."

²⁸ After she had said this, she went back and called her sister Mary aside. "The Teacher is here," she said, "and is asking for you." ²⁹ When Mary heard this, she got up quickly and went to him. ³⁰ Now Jesus had not yet entered the village, but was still at the place where Martha had met him. ³¹ When the Jews who had been with Mary in the house, comforting her, noticed how quickly she got up and went out, they followed her, supposing she was going to the tomb to mourn there.

³² When Mary reached the place where Jesus was and saw him, she fell at his feet and said, "Lord, if you had been here, my brother would not have died."

³³ When Jesus saw her weeping, and the Jews who had come along with her also weeping, he was deeply moved in spirit and troubled. ³⁴ "Where have you laid him?" he asked.

"Come and see, Lord," they replied.

³⁵ Jesus wept.

³⁶ Then the Jews said, "See how he loved him!"

³⁷ But some of them said, "Could not he who opened the eyes of the blind man have kept this man from dying?"

³⁸ Jesus, once more deeply moved, came to the tomb. It was a cave with a stone laid across the entrance. ³⁹ "Take away the stone," he said.

"But, Lord," said Martha, the sister of the dead man, "by this time there is a bad odor, for he has been there four days."

⁴⁰ Then Jesus said, "Did I not tell you that if you believe, you will see the glory of God?"

⁴¹ So they took away the stone. Then Jesus looked up and said, "Father, I thank you that you have heard me. ⁴² I knew that you always hear me, but I said this for the benefit of the people standing here, that they may believe that you sent me."

⁴³ When he had said this, Jesus called in a loud voice, "Lazarus, come out!" ⁴⁴ The dead man came out, his hands and feet wrapped with strips of linen, and a cloth around his face.

Jesus said to them, "Take off the grave clothes and let him go."

Acts 9:1–19

¹ Meanwhile, Saul was still breathing out murderous threats against the Lord's disciples. He went to the high priest ² and asked him for letters to the synagogues in Damascus, so that if he found any there who belonged to the Way, whether men or women, he might take them as prisoners to Jerusalem. ³ As he neared Damascus on his journey, suddenly a light from heaven flashed around him. ⁴ He fell to the ground and heard a voice say to him, "Saul, Saul, why do you persecute me?"

⁵ "Who are you, Lord?" Saul asked.

"I am Jesus, whom you are persecuting," he replied. ⁶ "Now get up and go into the city, and you will be told what you must do."

⁷ The men traveling with Saul stood there speechless; they heard the sound but did not see anyone. ⁸ Saul got up from the ground, but when he opened his eyes he could see nothing. So they led him by the hand into Damascus. ⁹ For three days he was blind, and did not eat or drink anything.

¹⁰ In Damascus there was a disciple named Ananias. The Lord called to him in a vision, "Ananias!"

"Yes, Lord," he answered.

¹¹ The Lord told him, "Go to the house of Judas on Straight Street and ask for a man from Tarsus named Saul, for he is praying. ¹² In a vision he has seen a man named Ananias come and place his hands on him to restore his sight."

¹³ "Lord," Ananias answered, "I have heard many reports about this man and all the harm he has done to your holy people in Jerusalem. ¹⁴ And he has come here with authority from the chief priests to arrest all who call on your name."

¹⁵ But the Lord said to Ananias, "Go! This man is my chosen instrument to proclaim my name to the Gentiles and their kings and to the people of Israel. ¹⁶ I will show him how much he must suffer for my name."

¹⁷ Then Ananias went to the house and entered it. Placing his hands on Saul, he said, "Brother Saul, the Lord—Jesus, who appeared to you on the road as you were coming here—has sent me so that you may see again and be filled with the Holy Spirit." ¹⁸ Immediately, something like scales fell from Saul's eyes, and he could see again. He got up and was baptized, ¹⁹ and after taking some food, he regained his strength.

www.ingramcontent.com/pod-product-compliance
Lightning Source LLC
LaVergne TN
LVHW022322080426
835508LV00041B/1746